Elva

Elva Boyd-Wilson

with
Shawn Smucker

Written by Shawn Smucker
Edited by Andi Cumbo (andilit.com) and Susannah Benson
Cover Design by Gentry Austin
Back cover photography by Nick Gould

This book is dedicated to

my parents who gave me confidence;
my husband Norris who loved me
and gave me a family to cherish;
my Clabell partners for the opportunity;
my wonderful employees, whose unwavering devotion
gives me the confidence to continue;
Sandy, who encouraged me to accept my success;

And most of all
to my children
Larry, Norris, and Laralee
and to the Divine Power who makes it all possible

CHAPTER ONE

I suppose in some ways the life I have today began when I was 39 years old. If that May day had never happened, I wonder where I would be right now? I wonder what my life would look like? Very different, I suppose. Very different.

It was 1958, and even though I'm 95 years old now the memory of that day is still clear in my mind. It's the day my world stopped. We lived in Maryland, on the Northeast River at Hances Point, a lovely summer community. May was that beautiful time of year when everything was a brilliant green or blue and heat came up off the trees in waves. It was a bustling time of the year as many of the families arrived for the summer, making their preparations and taking their boats out of storage.

Norris was president of the shipyard at Port Deposit, Maryland, on the Susquehanna River. They built more than boats, though – they did things like create tunnel sections and then ship them all over the world, first down the river and then through the Chesapeake Bay. Glen Wiley had created a revolutionary "Wiley Whirley" crane, and the shipyard, which bore his name, was known for innovative designs and features.

Once, Mr. Wiley himself was at the shipyard and a crowd of people watched as one of his huge Wiley cranes was being used. I guess the man operating it wasn't doing such a great job, and my husband spoke up, perhaps a bit too loudly.

"I guess if I couldn't do a better job than that, I'd climb down and stop trying," Norris said.

Mr. Wiley overheard him.

"You think you can do a better job than that?"

"I guess I could," Norris said.

"Well, then go ahead," Mr. Wiley said. To his surprise, Norris climbed up into the crane and did just that. That was just the kind of guy my husband was.

Most of the houses at Hances Point were on the river side, looking out over the water. There were tennis courts, too, and the summer cottages were owned by people who were pretty well off and had good jobs or owned businesses. Their children mostly went to private schools, but in the summer they'd come and make their home at Hances Point. We were a fairly isolated little community, so you ended up with all of these kids who were captive and couldn't go anywhere. They became great friends to us, and that was always the best part of the year, the green summer time, when Hances Point was full of families and there were children running around everywhere.

Everything the kids did in the summer was done as a pack. They roamed around Hances Point looking for fun, and it was a great place for children to grow up because if anyone did anything out-of-line, everyone found out about it and you could bring them back in line. Summer was an excellent time to have a birthday. One birthday cake was never enough, and everybody came. The birthday boy or girl was king or queen for the day.

Norris and I had three children: Larry, Laralee and Norris. Sometimes groups of kids would convince a parent to take them to the movies, and they'd load up a station wagon and head out. It seemed like everyone had a boat, so the kids were out on the water all the time, water-skiing or swimming off the dock. Our house had a long row of steps that led down to a pier, and at one time we had three boats docked there, their names painted on the side: Puzzle I, Puzzle II, and Puzzle III.

When I first met Norris, he was electrifying the Pennsylvania Railroad from Philadelphia to Pittsburgh, but by the time we got married, he was anticipating the next big job with Arundel Corp out of Baltimore. We were married in the summer, and he was unemployed, working on his father's family dairy farm. So one night we got together with some of his friends. Apparently, they had never heard of the name Elva before, and one of the young men tried to get my attention. He stumbled over my name, "Ella, uh, Eva, whatever, I can't remember that name. I'm just going to call you Puzzle."

I guess because my name was a puzzle to him. And that name stuck.

Norris named his boats after me, which was a huge compliment because he was into his boats. He had a mechanic in Northeast, a small town not too far away, who specialized in boats, so Norris's racing boat would go there during the week, and he spent quite a few nights up there working on the boat. He'd get home at 1 or 2 a.m. and climb into bed, leaving greasemarks on the sheet, then he'd wake early, clean himself up, and head into work.

On the weekends, he'd put the boat on a trailer and travel to different meets in the area, racing the boat and hanging out with the other boat folks in the racing circuit. At least that's what Norris and Larry did – I usually stayed home with the two younger children because there wasn't much for them to do at those races, and if I did take them I spent most of my time chasing them around or worrying that they'd end up in the water. If we didn't go, the day seemed endless and I'd walk up and down the road, worrying about them because there was a former participant who attended these races and he was missing an arm. .

On the afternoon that my entire life changed, the afternoon I'll never forget, Norris got home from work and hurried through the house. I was getting dinner ready for the five of us, and he shouted down from upstairs where he was changing his clothes.

"Put dinner on the table! I've got to get that boat out on the water before the sun goes down."

When the sun went down it got windy, and if it was already windy then it got a lot more windy. The weather always fluctuated around sunset. Plus, Norris had a meet coming up that weekend at our local yacht club, something he had arranged and had been quite a coup for him. A nationally accredited meet was being put on for his honor, a first for the club. He wanted to make a good showing with this new boat. It was a hydroplane, and there were various places on it that you could add weight to adjust the way it moved in the water. It was a pretty sensitive thing.

"I've got to get the boat out," he said again as he came downstairs.

"I'm frying chicken," I said, not looking up. "It's not really done."

"I don't care whether it's done or not," he said quickly. "Put it on the table. Let's eat."

Well, he kept insisting so I took the chicken off of the stove and we all sat down and ate. The chicken was really undercooked – I don't think I even ate all of mine.

"So who's taking Norris to baseball practice?" I asked, but I already knew the answer to that.

"I guess you are," he said. "I've got to get this boat out before the sun goes down."

"Okay, okay," I said. "Who's going to bring him home?"

He took another bite, then shrugged.

"Well, I guess we'll see," he said.

Norris gulped down his almost-done fried chicken then dashed out the door with Larry. They had the boat on a trailer and drove it down to the boat works, leaving me with Norris and Laralee.

I took Norris Jr. to baseball practice.

I wasn't there with them at the riverside, but later on someone told me about how things happened. They put the boat out in the water and Larry took it out first, the engine screaming, the water churning behind him. When he came back around and offered to let his father take it for a spin, Norris shook his head.

"You take it out again, son, it's too much for me."

That's what he said, anyway, but the truth was he wasn't feeling well. So Larry started it up again and flew out into the river. They had laid out a course, and Larry was trying it out. Norris watched from a small floating dock, his legs hanging over the side. Everyone on the shore had their eyes on this new racing boat as it flew through the water, kicking up foam. No one was watching Norris. Why would they have been watching him? He was just sitting there.

Later someone would tell me that it was around this time that Norris laid back on the barge, resting his head on its wooden surface. He muttered something to himself, something that sounded like,

"I have a terrific headache."

But I wasn't there when that happened. My son Norris had baseball practice in Northeast which was just four miles away, so I took him there. There was another mother there that I knew, so I stayed and we waited together for the kids. It was just for an hour or so, and I figured I might as well take my son home – his father would be busy on the boat and probably wouldn't want to pull himself away. It wasn't long before we were headed for home, and I dropped Norris Jr. off at the boatyard on my way by.

I clearly remember walking into the house. The sun would have been getting low on that May afternoon as the days stretched into summer. I walked into the house, and that's when I heard the phone ringing and ringing and ringing.

I picked it up.

"Elva, is that you?"

"Yes," I said. "Who is this? What's wrong?"

"Get down here to the boatyard. Something's wrong with Norris."

I hung up the phone with a clang and ran out the door. I drove as fast as I could down the narrow street to the small boatyard at the edge of Hance's Point, where all the boating activity took place. I got down there in a few minutes.

It really was a beautiful evening, and the wind had never gotten that bad. I thought of the man who had lost his arm – what would I do if that had happened to Norris? How would I take care of him? Would he still be able to boat even if he was seriously injured? My mind raced all over the place during that short drive to the water.

Most people used that little float to transport things to their boats, loading it from the dock. That's where Norris was when I first saw him, prone on the float, just lying there, not moving. There was an ambulance on the small road that ran along the boatyard, and as I ran down towards it they climbed on to the float, then loaded Norris into the back of the ambulance.

"That's my husband," I said, shocked, sort of stumbling towards all of that activity. Everything seemed to move in slow motion. I looked around for Larry. I'm not sure where Norris or Laralee were. The trees were so green, the sky a deepening blue. The day was ending and shadows stretched out into the water.

"Climb into the back," the ambulance driver said. "I'm the only one on duty today, so I'll need you to hold his oxygen in place while we drive to Elkton."

I nodded, lifted my dress, and climbed into the back of the

ambulance. Norris didn't move. His eyes stayed closed. I grabbed the oxygen mask and held it over his mouth and nose, and we pulled away from the river, turned around, and raced up the road, the sirens screaming.

CHAPTER TWO

I was born Elva Lowry, the daughter of George Lowry and Edna May Barnes. My father had four brothers and a sister. My mother had one sister whose birth had resulted in the death of their mother. They were just young people, my parents – neither one of them went to high school, but how could any amount of education have prepared newlyweds for the Great Depression? Still, they were married in the late teens, so they had a little bit of time to find work and buy a home.

Memories. Where do they go? How can you unearth the earliest ones? Some memories are so deep inside of you that you don't even know they're there, especially the ones from over ninety years ago. Those seem like they took place in another life, or in a dream. So long ago. Yet in an instant they flash to the surface – it doesn't take much. The touch of a particular fabric. The rough feel of a protruding thread. The smell of woodsmoke.

My mother worked at home tipping umbrellas. There was a big umbrella factory in Lancaster, Pennsylvania, and a busy little fellow came to our house in Columbia once a week, bringing her a bundle of umbrellas and the mechanisms that made them work. The umbrella cover itself was sewn with a machine in the factory in Lancaster, but there was a little place you had to pull the frame through and then sew it together by hand so that you could raise the umbrella. That was called tipping, not done in the factory but by people like my mother, by hand, and often in their homes.

So this man came with his bundle of umbrellas, a new bunch under his arm, and he'd take the umbrellas my mother had already finished. I remember her sitting in the house, focused, tipping one umbrella after another. I watched her thread the needle. I watched her long, slow sewing motion, the way she extended her arm and pulled the thread tight. The way she held the end of the thread in her teeth while she tied a small knot.

Meanwhile, my father worked in one of the iron mills there around Columbia. They called the one he worked in a "rolling mill" because they rolled huge bars into thinner, reinforced steel bars that came out about as big around as your finger. My father was the night engineer, a job that didn't require any particular type of schooling. His job was to keep the engine ready through the night so that they could really fire it up when the men arrived in the morning.

In one of my earliest memories, my father would take me out back behind the house on Houston Street. I was tiny, and from my perspective he was a solid rock, an unchanging mountain. If my father exhibited signs of his illness in those years, I didn't notice. We went into the back yard, and from there he could see across the field to the factory where he worked, the huge smoke stacks rising up into the sky, a sign of the industrial age just around the corner. My father could tell how busy he would be that night by the amount of smoke coming out of the boilers, into the stacks.

My father tended to swear a little, so sometimes when we looked across the field (with me perched on his shoulders or standing beside him, holding his hand), and when he saw huge bellows of smoke belching out of the smokestacks, my father would shake his head at the thought of the busy night of work he had ahead.

"I'm a son of a bitch," he'd mutter to himself. "Take a look at that smoke."

So one day, the two of us once again scouted out the mill to try to forecast my father's workload for the coming night, we watched the smoke billow out of the stacks. I could barely talk, but I was good at repeating what I heard, and I knew there was something significant about the rolling mill when the smoke came out in massive clouds.

"Daddy," I said, "Look at that tonabitch smoke."

It's a story that makes me chuckle. It's an image in my mind that makes me smile, that of a tiny girl standing beside her factory-working father, copying him.

In another one of these deeply buried memories, I lay on a small bed in the modest, two-story, attached house in Columbia, Pennsylvania. I was very young, maybe two or three years old, and I had been put down for a nap. The room was quiet, the light dim. A quilt covered the bed, but instead of being made out of ordinary quilt patches, it was made of velvets and heavy upholstery pieces with fancy stitches. I lay there on the bed and traced the pattern with my tiny fingers. That's the image in my mind: my tiny fingers. If I close my eyes, I can still feel those patches, those seams. Fabrics, yarns, and their application have always fascinated me.

The door had a square lock on it, the kind you pushed in to lock the door from the inside. It made a solid clicking sound when you locked it. The room was small, and the door was one of those old, sturdy, wooden doors surrounded by a broad frame. I eased myself out of the bed and toddled across the wood floor. I pushed in the lock – click – I guess I wanted to be alone. Or maybe I was simply bored, looking for places to go, things to push on.

The memory's next scene has me sitting on the bed, staring at the door where my parents are pleading and encouraging me to unlock the door.

"Elva, are you listening? Come over to the door. Elva? Please unlock the door."

But I didn't do it. Did I not understand what they wanted me to do? Was I being bullheaded? I'm not sure, but I laid my head back on my pillow and nearly went back to sleep. That's when my father appeared in the window, peering in at me and shaking his head.

There was an alley between us and the house to the left, and he had borrowed a ladder from the owner to climb up to free me! I don't think my parents were hard on me for locking the door. At least, I don't remember any ensuing discipline. I was an only child for most of my childhood, and my parents both treated me very well.

The house that joined ours to the right held a large Catholic family, whose name was Rendler. I spent some time in their house. Their girls were teenagers and I would watch them fix their hair and get ready to go to church. They treated me like a toy; besides that, I don't remember having much interaction with them, but years later, I got reacquainted with Mary, one of the girls, and our relationship was very pleasant.

My mother was a worrier by nature, perhaps because my father was not a robust man. Maybe it was because she lost her mother at such an early age, or maybe worrying was just part of her nature. She was consumed with the idea that I was getting ill, and she often got down on her knees beside me while I sat in my rocking chair.

"Elva, do you feel well?" she asked me, concern in her eyes. "Does it hurt anywhere?"

I got so sick of her asking me if I felt well that I'd shift the chair around so I didn't have to look at her. I remember that quite clearly, jerking the rocking chair to the side, moving so that she was behind me, and then rocking even faster, my little chin up in the air.

I could never convince her, though, that I was just fine. She was always taking me to doctors, always asking them about strange symptoms I wasn't even exhibiting, always trying to get me on medication. When traditional doctors weren't helping her peace of mind, she started taking me to less reputable healers.

I remember one in particular. She took me to an old man to be "measured," a Pennsylvania Dutch superstition. I can't remember exactly how old I was, but I was old enough to be embarrassed by a strange man lifting up my undershirt, his cold fingers wrapping a string around my abdomen. Then he took the string over the stove, lifted the lid off one of the burners, and the thin string lit into a line of flame before writhing and burning into a charred piece of black. That was the ritual – I don't know what it meant or what it was supposed to accomplish, but my mother seemed strangely relieved after she had me "measured." At least for a short time – then the usual worrying ensued.

There was a deep vein of superstition in those back alleyways and sidestreets of Columbia, PA, in those days. Men and women always looked for signs of things to come, and children peered through dark windows, wondering what supernatural power might be at work. Black cats and walking under ladders and opening an umbrella indoors brought bad luck. Breaking a mirror brought seven years of it. But there was nothing that couldn't be undone by turning in a circle seven times, or rubbing someone's lucky rabbit's foot.

We moved down the street when I was six, to a nicer house with a front porch. Our neighbors on one side had two sons. I don't remember my parents having many friends in those days – I don't think anyone did, really. They spent all the time they had working, eating, or sleeping. There wasn't much time for socializing.

But there were some nights when people would gather next door. They congregated at night, and there was talk about spells and hexes that people had put on each other, how one had led to sickness, how another had led to a mysterious death. Someone else's food had spoiled, the obvious result of an unhappy, spiritually powerful neighbor. Stepping over a broom handle in an open doorway was an invitation to the spell caster

One of the brothers would go down into the basement and bring up a pitcher of homemade wine, and the men would continue talking, telling stories that kept me wide awake at night. I never said a word – just sat there in the shadows in the kitchen, soaking it all in.

My father was normally quiet, and he didn't get as worked up about all of that stuff as my mother did, but they both wondered about the two spinster women who lived in the house on the other side of ours. They were old, those two women, but sturdy. They had a big garden and a large yard, and sometimes I watched them working, wondering why I wasn't allowed to take any of the fruit they offered me. Both women were very kind to me, and they kept their gray hair up in tight buns. They had cherry trees and peach trees, and sometimes they left fruits and vegetables from their garden on the ledge of the fence to ripen, but I was under strict instructions not to even touch it. Who knows what it would do to me? Make me sick? Turn me into a frog?

Sometimes I think all of that stuff just gave people something to talk about, something to believe in, some sense of control over their lives during a time when everything seemed to be spiraling out of control. We wanted to know that there was a reason that things happened the way they did, why a neighbor's wife died young or their child drowned or their parent got ill. Work and money were hard to come by. We never starved, but we never had a huge amount of anything left over, either. These superstitions and beliefs in the supernatural helped everyone feel like things could be explained, and perhaps even controlled.

Times were tough as we lived through the Depression, but my

father managed to sell that house and he bought a much smaller place downtown, just a shell of a house, but he was a "handy" man. He went into it with a garden hose and stripped layer after layer of wallpaper. He even electrified the house, making it one of the first houses on the block to have electric power. We had a radio, one of those with three knobs on the front, and when there was a prize fight the neighbors would gather out on the sidewalk and he'd turn it up so that everyone could hear. Everyone would cheer and shout and shush each other.

"Quiet now! What did he say? Who won that round?"

My brother was born while we lived in a rented house, waiting for my father to finish work on the place downtown. They called it a "high-step" house: there were steps on the outside that led up to the front door, and under those steps were doors that went down into the basement. On the 4th of July we'd have firecrackers, the kind that were all attached to a long, single fuse. We'd sit there under the steps and when people walked by we lit them and threw them out, laughing hysterically when they jumped in surprise.

The family who lived next to our "high-step" house were Catholic, and they had a big family. The mother was like a mother hen, and everyone (including me) ran to Oneida when they had a problem, which came in handy later in my life. After my father died and my step-father, an alcoholic, came after me and hit me, I would run to Oneida for help.

But that comes later in the story.

CHAPTER THREE

Mother gave up umbrella tipping and went to work at the sewing factory, where my father's sister and mother worked. It was walking distance from our house. I guess my father became my babysitter when she did that, because there weren't any kindergartens or day care centers in those days – nothing like that!

He took me for walks through the downtown area. Sometimes we'd stop in a pool room. They weren't very busy during the daytime, but the ones who were there would make a fuss over me.

Father would buy me a candy - they had a box of vanilla chocolates that cost a penny each. You broke them open and they were normally white inside but if you got a pink one you got a prize. My father lifted me up so that I could pick my chance out of the box – it was all rather exciting.

On other days, when it was sunny and warm, we spent time in the back yard. My father, always working with iron and steel and massive furnaces at night, emerged during the day to plant soft-colored flowers along the fence rows. It seems a rather great discrepancy, the factory worker on his knees, pulling back the warm earth, planting seeds and bulbs and pulling weeds. But he did, and each spring the flowers came up, and we always had tomatoes, radishes, beets, beans, and other vegetables. He also grew celery and put it in bunches which I sold from door to door.

I don't ever remember being spanked, and for most of those early years my father was my only playmate. He bought me a BB rifle for Christmas one year, although I don't have clear memories of using it. When the river froze over, he was the one to buy some of those skates you clamp on to your shoes. He tried to teach me to ice skate right there on the Susquehanna River. I wasn't a quick study when it came to ice skating, so he gave up.

In the afternoon, while we waited for mother to come home, I had this little game that I played by myself. In those days people bought insurance policies for ten cents a week, and the insurance man came around every week with a big leather book under his arm, collected the insurance money, and kept track of it in his ledger. I thought this was fascinating, so I played "insurance man." Mother had a chair in each of the four corners of the living room. I unloaded my piggy bank and put money in each seat, then I'd go around collecting on the policies and "making change." I have a feeling I might have been a pest with the piggy bank.

The summer before I started school, when I was five, my father took me on hikes into the countryside and we collected horseradish roots and wild cherries that he used to make wine. It was a good summer, and my father was very kind to me. Then in September I started school – I wouldn't turn six until February. It's funny to think about now, but even though I was only five years old, I walked to school. Everyone did.

It was a nice school, a large brick building on 9th street that had four main rooms. The sewing factory where my mother worked was maybe eight blocks away from our house, and the women walked home for lunch. All of the children at school walked home for lunch, too – you weren't allowed to take your lunch to school unless you received special permission. Sometimes, if I got home for lunch before my mother, I'd get the key from under the doormat and let the draft open on the coal stove so that mother could make something hot for lunch when she got back.

Those were different times, when a six year old walked back and forth by herself through the city to school and then walked home for lunch and got the stove ready. But in those days everyone had to pitch in, even from an early age. The whole family had to contribute, if you were going to make it.

My father sold the house we lived in and we moved down closer to a different iron mill, which meant I transferred to a different school in fourth grade. This was a big school with three rooms for each grade – I remember walking through there thinking, *This is the largest building I've ever walked through in my entire life.*

I wouldn't say I was scared, but I was certainly intimidated by the massive hallways, the seemingly endless row of doors. I walked timidly into my room and there were four names on the board: Janet, William, Dorothy, and Newcomer.

Well, isn't that nice? I thought to myself. *The teacher is welcoming me, the new comer, along with those other three children.*

But it turns out that was their family name. Newcomer. Oh, well.

My brother was born just before we moved to that house, and we lived across the street from a Catholic school attached to the church. When it was time for him to go to school, mother decided he could go to the Catholic school and that would be easier for him than walking to the one I went to, six blocks away.

But he didn't go there for very long. The sisters were tough on him, and one time when he wanted to go to the bathroom, he raised his hand.

"Charlie, stop it. Put your hand down," the nun told him.

He put his hand down for a few minutes, but he really had to go to the bathroom, so after a little while he raised his hand again.

"Charlie, stop it! You don't have to go," the nun said.

So he pooped his pants.

The nuns got even more upset about this, and when mother found out she gave those nuns a real earful and put Charlie in public school. It all seemed like a very big deal at the time. I guess that's life in a small town.

I suppose I was pretty smart in school, and I did well considering I didn't get much encouragement or support from my parents. My mother seemed impressed by my good grades, and I didn't think my father was particularly concerned either way, but I still ended up 20th in a class of 101. But that was in high school; in my earlier years, in elementary school, I wasn't sure where I fit in.

My fourth grade teacher, Miss Overland, asked me a question one day, and apparently she didn't like my answer.

"Well, that's a scatterbrained answer, Elva."

Scatterbrained? I thought to myself, and that sort of stuck with me for a little while. I wondered if I wasn't very smart. I wondered what a scatterbrained person could do with their life. But about that time the IQ test first came to our school. We were given the test in a large room, and the teachers milled around to make sure you weren't cheating. I ended up with two or three teachers standing behind me because I was getting through the test too fast. They didn't talk to me, but I could feel their eyes focused on the back of my head.

I found out later that my score had been that of a freshman in high school, something which helped me overcome the label of "scatterbrained" that Miss Overland had so quickly tagged me with.

So, there I was, growing older. I had a little brother and parents who worked hard to make ends meet for us. I had a pretty nice house, at least for those days, and I was getting an education. But the Depression deepened, and things became uncertain.

This uncertainty wasn't relegated to the outside world – it infiltrated my own house in the form of my father becoming increasingly sick. The pain in his chest was getting worse, and we didn't have any money for him to go to the doctor. Life was about to change.

CHAPTER FOUR

Once the Great Depression set in, my father didn't always have work – sometimes the mill closed down for a few days or a few weeks, and the families depending on the mill had to scrape and scratch to get by. The crazy thing was, even when my father worked, it didn't mean he would get paid. The mills simply didn't have the cash all the time to pay their workers (because their customers couldn't always pay them), so they sold iron or whatever else they sold on credit to their customers and continued producing even when they didn't get paid, which meant they couldn't pay their employees.

More than a few Saturdays, especially after my father got sick, word would get out that the mill could finally make some pay.

"Elva, walk out the tracks to get my pay," he'd say from the bed.

So I walked down the tracks with the other mill workers. The group walked slowly along the train tracks that ran through Columbia, rocks clattering among the rails. Little Elva walked in that crowd of twenty or thirty gruff and strong mill workers, not another woman in sight. I can't imagine that happening today, but back then I was perfectly safe – those men knew and loved my father, and they looked out for me. They were very respectful of me. I never had any sense of being in danger, not in spite of their presence, but because of their presence.

At the mill we'd wait outside the door and eventually the pay master came out with a wad of envelopes in his hand. He was a stumpy man with a big, fat lip, and he wiped his thumb along his lip to moisten it, then used his thumb to page through the pay envelopes and call out the men's last names. Sometimes he had money for all the men, and sometimes he could only pay a few of them.

Not too many years later that very same pay master killed himself. The strain of having those men work for money, be owed money, need the money, and then not have it to give them, I guess it was just too much. I can't remember how he did it, but I know that everyone in the neighborhood kind of understood why he did it. He had a job that no one else wanted, and you couldn't say that about too many jobs in the '30s.

"Mr. Lowry!" the pay master shouted, squinting his eyes and looking out over the crowd. Some of the men around me motioned that I was there to pick up my father's pay, so he gave the envelope of cash to one of the men in the front row, and they passed it back until it got to me. There was something significant in that, something about all of those men touching an envelope of cash and, even in their great need, passing it back to a small girl waiting to carry it home to her father. I felt that envelope and sighed with relief that we were getting money that week. I probably thought of the food it would buy, or the small amount of school supplies that I needed.

I waited patiently until all the envelopes had been passed out, and then we'd all walk back the railroad tracks together, maybe a ten-minute walk. I don't remember the group being very loud, although I suppose some of the men spoke to each other during the short trek back into the heart of the town. Once on our street, I'd run the rest of the way, eager to show the money to my father.

Meanwhile, school went on. For the most part, I enjoyed school, although it did come rather easy for me. Now that so many years have passed, I don't remember many of my teachers anymore, but I do remember my geography teacher in seventh grade: she was also the principle, and she was quite a disciplinarian. She had the reputation that, if something didn't suit her, she'd bring you up and put you over her knee. If you were a girl, she'd lift up your skirt to paddle you.

I was a bright girl, and I always raised my hand. Always. I enjoyed participating in the class, although I'm sure my eagerness occasionally came across as wanting to be teacher's pet. One particular morning I raised my hand for every question and she never called on me. Maybe she was in a bad mood that day, I don't know. But I kept raising my hand and she kept overlooking me.

Well, that's not entirely true. She overlooked me until she asked a question I wasn't sure about. I didn't raise my hand. Then she called on me.

"Elva?" she asked, and there was a glimmer of pleasure in her voice that she had caught me out. "Do you know the answer to the question?"

I didn't know. I just sat there for a moment. If you didn't know an answer, you had to stand up and say, "I don't know." I'm not sure I ever had to do that before.

So I stood up.

"I don't know the answer to that question," I said.

"Well, Elva," she said in a smug voice. "You don't know very much this morning, do you?"

I felt the color rush to my face, but I couldn't keep quiet. I couldn't let her sit there and insult me. Maybe this was the beginning of my courage, I'm not sure, but the incident sticks out so clearly in my mind.

"I knew the answer to every question you asked," I blurted out. "But you didn't call on me until I didn't know an answer."

Everyone in the class held their breath – you didn't talk back to teachers in those days, and you certainly didn't talk back to the geography teacher who was also the principal. That was simply asking for trouble.

As soon as the words came out of my mouth, I knew I was probably going to get a spanking. She was little and stubby and plush. She looked like a pie woman. But she ran the show, and I thought I was going to pay for my indiscretion. I could see her face harden, and I knew she was considering her options.

Then a new thought entered my head, something I had never considered before in my childhood.

I'm not going to let her paddle me. She is going to want to paddle me, but I won't let her.

I glanced down at my geography book. It was for the 7th and 8th grade, and it was thick and heavy.

If she comes towards me, I'm going to throw that book at her.

We stared at each other. The room was completely silent. My eyes had suddenly opened to the fact that you don't have to just sit there and take what comes – you can fight it. You can create your own life.

This all happened in a moment.

"All right," she said quietly. That was it. No verbal admonishment for talking back. No calling me to the front of the room. No more embarrassment.

I sat down, trembling. She must have known. Somehow she sensed that I wasn't going to take it from her. I don't know that I was a belligerent kid, but I wasn't going to let anyone make a fool out of me. I think that little incident gave me a huge boost of confidence, a belief that I could take care of myself, and I could stand up to adults if I had to.

My mother made a mustard plaster, like a paste, and laid it on my father's back. It was smooth and strong and was supposed to draw out the deep pain, but it often burned his back, left it red and raw.

"It's not strong enough," he said quietly, grimacing under the pain. "Make it stronger."

So she'd mix up another batch and he'd lie there and she'd spread the thin mixture on a white piece of scrap cloth and he'd be there for an hour or two, hoping the mustard plater would draw out whatever needed to be drawn out. The pain in his chest was getting worse, and we couldn't afford for him to go to the doctor – we barely had money for food and the other bills that came in. I don't know if they saved up money or how they did it, but eventually they got him in to see a doctor.

"It's an inflamation in the lining of the heart," the doctor told them. Myocarditis. If they would have had money for a doctor, he could have had the proper medication, but they didn't have any money so my mother and father put a bed down in the living room so he wouldn't have to climb the stairs, and that's where he stayed most of the day. That was in the fall, when the air was cooling and the leaves were changing and you could see the "tonabitch" smoke pouring from the smoke stacks at the rolling mill. It was a long autumn, a slow passing of days with a father in a bed in the living room, dying.

My father wanted to have a nice Christmas. He knew he didn't have long to live. So he went to the bank and borrowed $1500 and told them he was going to build a garage in the back yard, but he didn't build a garage. We had a Christmas. He bought a turkey for Christmas dinner and bought my brother a bicycle. I don't even remember what he got me, but I remember it was a bittersweet feeling, having such a nice Christmas with my father sleeping on a bed in the living room, dying. We used the rest of the money to live on.

Then the New Year came and winter set in, and he got worse, and because we couldn't afford a doctor his last days were terrible. Awful days. He died in February, the dead of winter, the time of year when it seems that spring will never come. Mother didn't have a cemetery plot, so someone suggested she go out to Ironville, and she found a church out there that sold her four plots for $15. That's where my father would be buried.

First there was the funeral at the funeral parlor in Columbia, and I remember one old lady staring at me with disapproval because I wasn't crying. She didn't know I wasn't a crier – I never cried when other people were around, not about anything. Besides, I had used up all my tears the night before. My mother's younger sister Aunt Betty had come in from Michigan just for the funeral. She bunked with me in my bed the night before the funeral, and we had cried together.

I always loved my Aunt Betty. She was a tiny little thing, and very pretty. She always had problems with men, but I didn't know nor care about that. I was just glad she was there. But even my Aunt Betty couldn't keep the funeral from happening, no matter how wonderful she was, and in the days to follow life returned to something like normal. My brother and I went back to school. The days passed, and the house felt empty. My little brother was just five years old, so he doesn't remember much about my father. I was nearly 14, a freshman in high school. Suddenly, it was just the three of us.

CHAPTER FIVE

It was the height of the Great Depression. My mother started getting $50 per month in Widow's Assistance, a government program that helped women who lost their husbands during that difficult time. When we received our first payment and instructions on how to report it, my mother threw her hands up in despair.

"I'll never be able to do all those numbers and make it come out right," she said, sitting down and sighing. It didn't take much to deflate her in those days after my father died. I'm pretty sure she never went to high school, so the numbers didn't come easy for her.

"Don't worry about it, Mother," I said. "I'll do it."

"What do you know about it?" she asked, giving me a strange look.

"Mother, the state doesn't care whether we get two quarts of milk and one loaf of bread, or two loaves of bread and one quart of milk. I'll make it come out right."

So I took over our finances, keeping track of everything and filling out the monthly reports that were required if she wanted to continue to receive her widow's allowance. Out of the $50, first we had to pay $15 per month to the bank on the loan my father had taken out to give us a good Christmas before he died. So we lived on $35 a month, and I had a spreadsheet where I would write in all the money we spent.

I was a freshman in high school, keeping track of our money, trying to keep an eye on my younger brother, and also beginning to consider my options for the future. During the semester my father died, I got an "E" in ancient history, the sort of grade you got that signified an "Incomplete." I always thought how unobservant that teacher was – he was the football coach. What kind of a teacher gives an incomplete to a girl who just lost her father and had always made A's before that?

As spring arrived, my brother, my mother and I watched all of my father's flowers grow along the fence rows. It made me sad, both because it was such a strong reminder of his absence, and also because none of us knew how to take care of them very well. Soon the flowers were choked with weeds, and I did my best to keep the little flower garden alive.

Mother also took special interest in the flowers, first walking over to the fence row and standing there, staring at the blooms. Eventually she would cut a few, then take them on the train to Ironville where she would lay them on the earth that covered my father's grave. But Mother met someone on the train, someone who would try to fill the emptiness left after my father's death.

One of the things young people did when my Mother was a girl was to stand around on street corners with their friends and sing. This would have been during the turning of the 19th into the 20th century, before the World Wars, before any of that. She grew up there in Columbia, and on summer evenings she sang with her friends. Sometimes people walking by would stop and listen.

When Mother started taking the train to Ironville, delivering fresh flowers to my father's graveside, she met one of her old singing friends. He had been part of their group, but the years hadn't been good to him. He had a drinking problem and was separated from his wife. I wonder when my Mother's trips to the cemetery became less about delivering my father's flowers and more about talking with the conductor of the train, this old friend of hers.

Shortly, he moved in with us and applied for a divorce from the woman he had married many years before, something that wasn't really done in those days. Respectable people didn't live together unless they were married, and I took some guff about it at school. Even one of my best friends gave me a hard time about this man living in our house, and it really hurt, coming from her. That was a strange time. We already felt different, not having a father, and when this man moved in with my mother, I felt even more like an outsider.

But once his divorce became final, my mother married him. It was a quiet affair. And our lives went on.

My step-father was a brutal, nasty man during my teenage years at home. When he was intoxicated, he would beat me, and I would run to a neighbor's house for safety. But in later years, when his medical condition forced him to stay sober, our relationship improved, and he grew to love me and my children as though we were his own.

But there in Columbia, well, his drinking was ugly. I started to think that he didn't understand me, that he didn't really understand how children worked. We couldn't be in the same room together without getting into a terrible argument over something, anything. But, on the other hand, he seemed pretty good with my brother. In fact, as my brother got older, he bought him a motorcycle, and the first time my brother drove it he wrecked it into a telephone pole and broke his collar bone.

That was the end of the motorcycle.

When my step-father wasn't drunk, he was fine, a relatively nice person. But he drank and drank until it got the best of him. Alcohol made him mean and nasty. Years later the doctor told him he couldn't drink anymore, that he would die soon if he didn't quit, and he was a pretty decent person after that. We still weren't best friends, but things around the house were more peaceful, less confrontational. I was a teenager by the time he quit drinking, and I was just about ready to leave home.

But when he was still drinking, we had some real knock-down, drag-out arguments, the kind that seemed to leave the house shaking. My mother didn't know whose side to take. She didn't know how to deal with it. I think if someone would have taken control of the situation, things could have been better between my step-father and me, but he kept drinking and I kept fighting with him. So when the summer arrived, she concocted a way to split my step-father and me. Well, I don't know, maybe that wasn't her intention, but it worked out that way.

"Why don't you go spend the summer with your aunt in Detroit?" she asked one day when school was nearly out. My step-father had moved into our house, and I was 15, looking to spread my wings a bit.

It was the best idea I had heard in a long, long time.

CHAPTER SIX

My Aunt Betty lived in Detroit. She was the same aunt who had shared my bed the night before my father's funeral, the same aunt who had wept with me until our pillows were soaked with our tears. I loved her desperately. My grandmother had died giving birth to her, and so my mother was 12 or 13 or thereabouts and she stopped going to school, stayed home to raise Aunt Betty and to run the house while their father worked.

Aunt Betty had a child who was a little older than me named Virginia, and she also had a daughter, Nancy, who was a little younger than me. She also had two boys, and sometimes she'd bring the entire family to stay with us. Aunt Betty and my mother were very close. They weren't very much alike, but they were sisters, and they shared the bond of growing up without a mother.

Because my step-father worked for the railroad, he could get me passes to travel by train to Detroit, so at the age of 15 I set out on my greatest adventure yet. I clutched my Reading Railroad pass and mother got the train with me from Lancaster to Reading. I remember standing on the platform there in Lancaster, looking down the long track every thirty seconds for signs of our arriving train, and when we got on I sat by the window and watched the countryside race past us: small towns and farmland, forests and valleys, streams and small country roads. Farmers worked in the fields and the small factories that had begun to crop up smoked, reminding me of my father.

Mother walked me from the Reading Railroad station to the Lehigh Valley Station – I would have to switch trains once by myself, in Buffalo, and mother couldn't stop giving me advice even after she had me on the train to Buffalo.

"Don't talk to strangers," she said. "And don't miss your train. Don't dawdle! And whatever you do, when you're changing trains in Buffalo, do not get into anyone else's automobile."

"Yes, Mother," I said, for the tenth time. I waved to her through the window, and the train pulled away.

I sat next to a kind woman on the train. She was traveling, too, and was in her 30s or 40s. I told her about who I was going to see and she told me all about her own trip, though I can't remember the details anymore. That leg of the trip went pretty fast. As we approached the station in Buffalo, she asked me where I was going.

"Once we get to Buffalo, I have to walk up the street to catch my train to Detroit," I said.

"When my family arrives to pick me up, you come with us. We'll drive you to the station," she said.

And she seemed so nice, so after we got off the train and collected our things, we walked outside together and waited along the sidewalk for her family. I thought nervously about my mother's last words to me.

"And whatever you do, when you're changing trains in Buffalo, do not get into anyone else's automobile!"

But I was my own person in those days, not one to follow rules for the sake of it, and the family seemed so nice, so I climbed into the car with them and they drove me up the street, dropping me off at the station. I felt rather grown up – not only was I traveling on my own all the way to Detroit, I was getting in and out of strangers' cars and doing just fine for myself, thank you very much!

My train ride to Detroit was uneventful, and when I got off the train, there was my Aunt Betty. I was so happy to see her, and she hugged me and hugged me, then took me to the car and we drove back to her house.

Aunt Betty's husband Joe, the father of her children, also lived in Detroit but they weren't together. My Uncle Joe had a live-in housekeeper, if that's what you want to call it, and Aunt Betty had a man that came and stayed quite a lot. I don't know whether or not he spent the night, but he was always there. Theirs was an interesting arrangement, not something I ever asked about or commented on. In Detroit it was live and let live.

Besides all the men that came around inquiring for my beautiful Aunt Betty, she also kept a Great Dane in the house named Jerry. He was a massive, great big animal, a truly wonderful dog. I took Jerry for walks and he wore a choke collar you could put your finger through. I never got very far before all the neighborhood children came running.

"Jerry!" they shouted from every direction. "Wait up, Jerry!"

The smallest children came out, children so little next to him that he could have been a horse for them to ride, and they wrapped their arms around his neck and ooh'd and aah'd. They kissed his face and stroked his back and I had to practically tug at him to get him to move along. But no matter how far we went from the house, the children knew Jerry and came running to greet him. He was practically a celebrity in that part of town.

One of my "jobs" that summer was to go buy Aunt Betty's meat at the butcher, and I always took Jerry along to the butcher's shop. Right inside the door, I stopped and looked at Jerry.

"Down, Jerry," I said in a stern voice. The first few times I took him in there, I was worried he might go crazy and start eating everything in sight. But he was a very good dog in the butcher shop, because he knew those visits ended in food for him, so he laid down until I purchased everything I needed and said it was time to go. Then he stood and walked out with me.

He was a different dog on the way home. On the way to the butcher shop, he lollygagged along, stopping for every child who wanted to pet him, meandering here and there and everywhere if you let him. But after the butcher shop? He was a dog on a mission. He walked right beside my hip without going left or right, and he wouldn't even stop for children unless I tugged on his collar, because he knew going home from the butcher meant I had bones for him once we got back.

Sometimes I let him run free, and he ran up to the street corner and then he waited to cross until I caught up with him. As soon as we got home he ran inside and we gave him the large bone from the meat. He was a good dog and one of the highlights of my wonderful trip to Detroit that summer.

Aunt Betty often took us out to the lakes – there were so many outside the city. I don't think anyone charged you anything to swim there, so we made up a lunch from whatever we could scrounge from the refrigerator. We chopped up some bologna and put onions and celery and stuff on there to make more out of it, and Uncle Joe's live-in made us tomato soup cake without icing, and it was so good. It tasted like spice cake.

We went out to the lake and spent the day on the beach, and my cousins and I ran into the water and back out again because it was so cold it took our breath away. The sky seemed stretched, far out over the water, and the small waves barely made a sound. You could hear children way down the beach, screeching and laughing. When we finally remembered the food, we took it out of the bag and ate it ravenously.

Then we just sat there on the shore and watched the sun. Life was good in Detroit. I wasn't sure I was ready to go home. When I did think of home, I thought of school, and my drunk step-father. I thought of the small row of flowers growing along the fence.

But it came time to go back, and I went through the same routine. I said good-bye to Jerry at the house. Before I got on the train in Detroit, I kissed Aunt Betty and hugged my cousins and I didn't really want to go home. Aunt Betty cried and made me promise to come see them again soon. From Detroit I took the train to Buffalo, but this time I had to wait in Buffalo for three or four hours, and it was night time.

There was no air conditioning in the train station, and all the windows were wide open. When I got to the ladies' waiting room, there was a man standing outside.

"Maybe I should come in and keep you company," he said. I blushed – he made me angry.

"You can't come in here," I blurted out. "It's the ladies' room."

When I turned around, there he was, standing in the doorway. Not doing anything, just standing there. I pushed past him and trotted over to the only other person in the station, the ticket seller. He was way on the other side of the station. I walked curtly up to his window.

"What can I do for you, miss?" he asked in a sleepy voice.

"Is that the ladies' room down the hall there?"

"Yes, ma'am, it is."

"Then you go down there and get that man out of it," I said.

His eyes opened wide and he hopped to it. I didn't have any more trouble with that man.

Finally I boarded my train for home. It went through the night, and I slept off and on as the train clacked over the tracks. Early in the morning I arrived back in Lancaster. I can't remember if I told my mother about everything I had seen or done. I can't remember if I told her about Jerry the Great Dane or the lakes or the city streets, so much bigger than Columbia. I can't even remember if I told her about the man in the bathroom.

Probably not. She probably asked me a few questions, and I most likely answered them without elaborating. That's just how it was between me and my mother. We never spoke much, and especially after she married my step-father we didn't seem to connect on very much.

My relationship with her (and my father, for that matter) was never a very demonstrative one, but I knew I was important to them. They simply weren't warm and cuddly people, and my Mother didn't change in this regard after my father passed away. But in later years Mother was always there when I needed her. She was always there for me when I brought my babies home from the hospital, and even though they lived near Allentown and we lived in Millersville, my step-father would bring her down to visit.

When I was growing up, she always made my dresses and helped me learn how to use her treadle sewing machine. I was soon doing my own sewing and, even as a teenager, embarked on a life-long love of knitting, crocheting, needlepoint – all of the needle arts. These talents, gifts from my mother, still play a big part in my life.

In fact, in 1979, I took 1st prize in the Annual Lancaster Needlework Show with a needlepoint I designed and created. It's now hanging in my daughter's living room in Florida. Another of my favorites was needlepoint rugs I made for a doll house for an oilman's wife that I met at Maine Chance. Doll houses were the girl's hobby and a treacherous storm had wreaked havoc on her collection. I urged her to send me sizes of some of the little rooms when she returned home from the spa, and I would produce some tiny rugs for her. I made several out of scraps of leftover yarn and mailed them to her in Texas.

Of course, she wanted to pay me for them, but it had been such fun for me, so I adamantly declined. She and her husband were traveling in Europe, and she was so delighted to communicate with me from the Hotel Lancaster in Paris. I got a package from her which contained a lovely scarf from a well-known designer. My decorator had it framed and hung it in the dining room of our home in Naples, Florida.

So many adventures and blessings, all because my mother taught me how to sew and instilled in me a love for needlepoint.

CHAPTER SEVEN

A few years passed. I graduated from high school in the commercial course, which meant I had taken some business preparation classes. I would have loved to go on to Lancaster Business College, but I would have needed my step-father to help with that financially and mother didn't really know how to handle our relationship. I think if she had been a little more astute, things wouldn't have been as bad as they were between my step-father and me. But it was what it was, and I didn't go any further in school.

Anyway, it was 1936, and there wasn't anything for anyone to do. School was out and my whole, seemingly endless future stretched out in front of me. But what was a girl to do in Columbia, Pennsylvania, the Great Depression still holding us down, the war in Europe starting to get our attention? Hitler was making headlines, as were the various other world leaders who tried to decide what to do in the face of his vocal aggression.

But my concerns weren't so broad or far-reaching. The highlight of that summer was when I could scrounge together ten cents and go to the swimming pool in Ironville.

One day my mother stood in the street talking with a few of the neighborhood women and someone told her that girls my age, and even younger, had gone to the local throwing plant and managed to get themselves hired. A throwing plant was basically a factory that processed textiles, turning yarn and other materials into a synthetic material. The raw material came into the factory, and you didn't have to be too smart to tie a knot in it and thread the spools.

Mother came back into the house.

"Elva," she said. "I hear there are some girls going down to that throwing plant and getting themselves hired. You should look into it."

I shrugged.

"They make 10 ½ cents per hour," she said.

10 ½ cents an hour didn't sound too bad.

"Okay, Mother, I'll look into it."

I was 17 years old that summer, and I couldn't think of what I would do with the money. My step-father had a good-paying job, so we weren't short of any necessities. If I had any extra money, I'd probably buy clothes and go to the swimming pool more often. I had never had a real job before that, but I walked down to the throwing plant the next day and was interviewed by an older man who ran the whole show.

He explained to me what went on in that particular plant. They received deliveries of raw rayon, a flat fiber, and spun it into yarn for stockings. Then he asked about me.

I told him how I had grown up in Columbia, how my father had worked in the iron mill, how I had graduated that spring from the commercial course in high school, and how my father had died.

He looked intrigued.

"Graduated from high school, eh?" he asked, looking at some papers on his desk. "So what makes you think you can do this job?"

As I grew older, I realized that I was actually a very confident person. I didn't back down to anyone – perhaps the first sign of this was the day I didn't back down from my geography teacher, the day I was ready to throw a book at her if she decided she was going to try and paddle me. That old man running the throwing plant didn't intimidate me at all.

"What makes me think I can do a good job?" I asked. "I've never tried to do anything with my hands that I haven't been able to do. I knit. I sew. I'm good with my hands."

He nodded and stared back at the desk covered in papers. I think he was impressed by my confidence, and I'm sure he pitied me for my lack of a father.

"Okay," he said suddenly, as if he had finally come to a conclusion about me. "We're not going to have you do what the other girls are doing. We'll make a spinner out of you."

I wasn't sure what that meant. I thought maybe he was trying to give me a lesser job.

"My mother said I would make 10 ½ cents if I came down here and did what those other girls are doing."

"You're mother's right. You would make 10 ½ cents an hour doing that. But we're going to make you into a spinner, and if you can catch on, after 6 weeks apprenticeship you'll get bumped up to 35 cents an hour."

My eyes went big. 35 cents an hour! That was serious money in those days. There were men supporting entire households on 35 cents an hour.

"Yes, sir," I said.

He smiled and leaned back in his chair, as if he had just made a very good decision.

"You can start tomorrow," he said.

I got up and turned to leave, but as I walked out the door he called one last thing to me.

"And no dresses!" he warned. "You have to wear pants."

When I showed up for my first day of work, another man, probably a foreman, gave me a tour of the area where I'd be working. I know I said not too long ago that I wasn't easily intimidated, but looking out over that massive piece of machinary, well, I may have had second thoughts about what I had signed up for.

They were huge, long machines that had fifty ends on each side. I was supposed to load a single spool on to each end (the spools were what the 10 ½-cents-an-hour girls made). When the spool came to the end, it stopped running and I had to replace it. There were 100 ends on each machine – 100 places to put a spool – and 18 machines to keep going. If you could keep all of the spools loaded and spinning, then you were "keeping your ends up."

It was a little dangerous because the thing that spun each spool was run by a belt that was always very tense and spinning quickly. When the spool emptied, there was a little eye in the machinary you had to get the thread through in order to start it back up again. This is why they asked us to wear pants and not dresses – you certainly didn't want to get caught up in one of those belts or you might get pulled into the machinary.

So I worked and I worked, and during those first six weeks I made 10 ½ cents an hour, just like the other girls. I spent my money on clothes, just like I thought I would, and I also bought my little brother his first suit. I don't know that I saved much of it – I didn't have much need for it, anyway. It was nice to have extra money for a change. There was one girl on the afternoon crew who was also a high school graduate, and she and I got on well and were friendly to each other.

You could hardly see me when I was working – I was so short next to those huge machines. I darted around, dodging the belts, respooling the ends. The whole thing was a dance, and the humming of the machine was the music. I got very good at it and soon was running the entire thing, keeping my ends up. I enjoyed it because it was a challenge and it kept me busy, and I liked the idea of having my own money to spend.

The Friday afternoon at the end of my six weeks, I went to the foreman.

"I go on full pay on Monday," I said. He didn't look up. He just kept studying whatever it was he was studying on his clipboard. Timecards, or productivity charts, or maybe nothing. Maybe he didn't want to deal with an overenthusiastic 17-year-old.

"I guess the superintendant will have to approve that first," he said elusively.

But I had grown a lot since the days my geography teacher called me out in front of the class. Besides, I had nothing to lose – if I lost my job for speaking up, then so be it.

"Have him approve it," I said sharply. "Or get somebody else to run these machines. I'm not going to run them for 10 ½ cents an hour after my training period is up."

He stared at me for a moment. On Monday they moved me up to 35 cents an hour.

CHAPTER EIGHT

In 1936 I was only allowed to work until 9 o'clock because I hadn't turned 18 yet. The regular shift went until 10pm, and there were a bunch of hard girls who ran the machines. Most of them were from Marietta, and they were tough, they really were. The first time I walked into the bathroom, a group of them stood in there smoking. They looked at me suspiciously, then one of them said something in a loud voice.

"Don't you sit down on these toilet seats," she said, exhaling smoke into the cloudy room. "They have crabs on them."

That was my introduction to them. They were rough, and they had probably encountered things in life that, at 17, I had no idea about.

The man who hired me knew that my father had died, and he checked in with me from time to time to make sure I was doing okay. On Friday nights he gave us our checks, and most of the girls went to a local bar to get their check cashed. Now I had to quit working at 9pm because I was only 17 years old, but they worked until 10, so I hung around until they got off and then went down to the bar with them to cash my check, too.

When the man who hired me found out I was going down to the bar with these rough girls from Marietta, he pulled me aside.

"I don't want you doing that," he said quietly. "Those girls are trouble, and you shouldn't be hanging out in bars at your age. You let me know when you have your check and I'll cash it for you."

So he started cashing my checks for me. He was a very nice gentleman. And then I went with the girls to the bar anyway! I was bored and 17 years old and I liked hanging out with those Marietta girls. There were probably around ten of them, and they were exciting to be around. Plus, if I hung out with them I didn't have to go home and face the possibility of my step-father being drunk.

One night, around 6pm, I noticed the plant was sending people home early. The superintendant did this sometimes, when there wasn't enough material to turn into spools, or if money was running tight (which, in those days, was most of the time). I saw one man walk along the outside of the factory on a night they sent some people home early. For some reason the superintendant hadn't sent me home – maybe he thought that since my father had died, my family needed the money.

The man walking outside stopped and looked in through the window at me, not in a mean way. He was just looking. But he had this look in his eyes and I knew he needed the work. He didn't want to go home – he wanted to keep working. I knew who he was – he had a family to provide for, kids to feed. I thought about how I'd probably spend my next check by going to the swimming pool or buying more clothing.

I walked straight over to the superintendant's office.

"Hey, don't you send him home and leave me here," I said. "I don't have anything I have to do with this money. That man has a family to keep."

He nodded.

"Okay."

After that, if someone needed to be sent home, it was me.

Those Columbia winters, spent in factories not far from the river, were bitter cold. Our house was heated with the wood stove in the kitchen, so going to bed meant wearing the warmest pajamas possible and crawling into a cocoon of blankets. It was hard to get out from under those blankets in the morning and walk through the dark and the cold to the factory. Plus, those first few winters after my father died reminded me of the last weeks of his life, the bed in the lviing room, our last Christmas, and his terrible death.

I ducked my head down and walked through that small city. The houses lined up in long rows, most of them brick with alleys running behind them. It was a nice place to live, and a lot of my extended family lived in the neighboring blocks. I certainly didn't know everyone – not even close – but Columbia was small enough that I was always seeing people I did know, and in those days you tended to know most of the people on your block pretty well.

The girl I worked with at the throwing plant, Dot, was also a high school graduate like me, and she suggested something that spring as the weather began to change and the water, frozen for so long, began to melt.

"Let's go to Atlantic City and get a job for the summer," she said. I thought that sounded like a wonderful idea, and I said as much.

"But how are we going to get there?" I asked.

"We'll get our boyfriends to take us," she said with a mischievous look in her eye, and we both laughed. We each had a boyfriend at that point, so we asked them and they agreed. The four of us double-dated, and a trip to Atlantic City was a fun way to spend a Sunday.

I don't think I talked to my mother about it very much – in those days, I did what I wanted to do, and my mother didn't have the personality to stand in my way. My step-father was probably rather happy to get me out of the house. We still didn't see eye to eye on anything. So I hopped in the car, and off we went to Atlantic City to live life and be young.

It felt incredible, driving down there,. Dot had some good leads on places that were hiring, and for some reason, even though it was only 1936 and the country was still reeling from the Great Depression, we were optimistic. Our boyfriends drove us into Atlantic City, and we got jobs there.

I can't remember how the two of us got split up, but somehow I ended up working at Chalfont and Hadden Hall, two of the nicest hotels in Atlantic City, and she ended up somewhere else. These two families, the Leeds and the Lippencotes, owned the two hotels – they were huge buildings, although I don't remember how many people could stay there. But they were big enough that the families also bought a few of the smaller hotels on the adjoining streets and used them to board us girls who worked for them.

They ran those places where we lived like a girls' boarding school. We had a matron, an intimidating woman we all knew was in charge, and if you arrived home after midnight you had to sign in and then go talk to her in the morning, explaining why you had been out after curfew. That was the last thing you wanted to do, and no one wanted to risk losing such a good job, so for the most part we kept to the curfew (except for in one instance, which I'll tell you about later).

We also had a black maid who looked after the common room where we all smoked and socialized. She was a kind woman who took excellent care of us. Many of the girls smoked back then – it seemed a right of passage. In the evenings that room was cloudy with smoke and the sound of girls' chatting voices. It was a fun place to live.

You could walk directly from that small boarding hotel into the kitchen at Chalfont, and if you were working at Hadden Hall you could go through a tunnel under the street. The owners were fair and ran a tight ship. They wouldn't hire anyone who didn't have a high school diploma or had waited on tables before. They said they didn't want to inherit anyone else's bad habits – they wanted to train their people from scratch, teach them how to do the job right.

We had a training period and we served the rest of the hired help in one of the dining rooms as practice. One of the hardest things was carrying the large trays down a long flight of stairs from the kitchen. There were a lot of dropped trays and missteps during training, but by the time they finished with you, you were a professional, upscale waitress. Once the summer season kicked in, you would take care of your assigned guests for as long as they were at the hotel, and then when they left they gave you a big tip for the entire time they had been there. It was a very nice place to work.

What a summer! What a place to cut my teeth on independence! It really was one of the best times of my life, working hard, meeting new people from all over, making new friends and living on my own. It felt good to get out of Columbia, to get out from under the cloud my step-father had brought to the house. I missed my little brother, and I missed my mother, but to be honest I was so busy that I rarely thought about it.

When the fall rolled around they put out a notice that anyone who had any commercial training (typing or accounting or things like that) was welcome to stay on through the winter and they'd continue our room and board. They'd try to get us into the dining room for tip money when they could – that's what gave us spending money to get our hair done and our nails done and to buy hose. So I decided to stay over the winter. To me, by then, Chalfont and Hadden had become home.

Soon, though, things would change. I would have laughed if anyone had told me that I'd be married within a year, but I guess we never can see what's just around the corner.

CHAPTER NINE

My time in Atlantic City was absolutely wonderful. I loved it there, especially because of the beach. I'd run down to the water any chance I got. We worked during mealtime hours, so after breafkast I'd grab my things and go hang out at the beach until lunch, when I'd race back to the Chalfont, get cleaned up, and wait on my tables. Then, after lunch, I'd go back to the beach, often spending the entire afternoon there until it was time to prepare for dinner.

I often went into the dining room with my hair wet from the ocean. I've lived along the water for a great deal of my life, and I wonder if my love for the water started during that summer I worked at Atlantic City. That time created inside of me a strong association between the water and freedom. Maybe it started even earlier, when I visited Aunt Betty in Detroit and she took me and my cousins to the lake. Whenever that love for the water started, it stayed with me through all of these years.

It wasn't just the beach that made my time in Atlantic City so special – working at the Chalfont and Hadden Hall meant we were a cut above. Our peers knew we worked there, and there was something special about it. Everyone wanted to work there; everyone wanted to be part of the Chalfont and Hadden Hall gang. So in Atlantic City I found some sense of belonging, too.

And the boys. Of course, there were a lot of boys.

The black boys were room service waiters, in uniforms, and there was definitely a separateness, a barrier between the whites and the blacks. This was 1937, after all, many, many years before Martin Luther King Jr., many years before the end of segregation. Less than 75 years after the Civil War. Imagine that.

They were all nice young men, the service waiters, and we all worked well together. Us waitresses always carried our own trays, and they were huge, brutal to carry, because there were so many courses for each meal, which added up to a lot of dishes. Plus we bused our own tables, clearing them when the meal was over and once again carrying everything back to the kitchen on those massive trays. If you got into where you unloaded the trays, and there was a service waiter there, he'd take it down off your shoulder for you. They called me Miss Elva.

"I'll take that for you, Miss Elva."

"Why, thank you!"

One day I walked into the common area and started talking with a black gal who worked as a maid in the hotels.

"These white girls, they want to meet the black boys at my house, Miss Elva," she said, shaking her head. "But I won't have any of that."

She was a little older than us, not quite old enough to be our mother, but perhaps a young aunt. I just smiled because I knew she was right – some of the girls did want to meet up with the black boys, and sometimes they did, with or without the maid's help. I'm not exactly sure why she was opposed to it – maybe she knew the girls would be in it deep with their parents if they hooked up with a black boy, or maybe she was concerned that some of the more racial elements in the city would put pressure on a young black man if he was seen around town with a white girl. There was so many layers regarding race back then, and the lines were drawn very clearly, and the owners of the hotels would not have condoned that.

I only ever had one problem with one of the service waiters.

We had a communal bathroom with four stalls and a shower and a row of basins. There was a big barrel by the door where you put your wet towel – I guess we weren't limited in towels. My room wasn't far from the bathroom, and one day I walked down there to brush my teeth. I was dressed all except my uniform – I had my undergarments on, my slip and panty hose and whatever else.

I leaned over and put my towel over the barrel so that I could reach out and get it. Before I knew what was happening, one of the black service waiters came in to empty the barrel of all the wet towels. He just stood there for a moment and stared at me, then leaned against the door frame.

"Whew, boy," he exclaimed, his eyes moving up and down my slip. He didn't look like he was going anywhere.

I bristled.

"You son of a bitch. If you ever talk to me again, I'm going to report you!"

I snapped my towel off the barrel and left, and no one ever gave me any trouble after that.

One of my close friends there in the house was a girl who was quite a bit older than me. Her name was Helen, and she was a beautiful girl, lots of fun.

The families who owned the two hotels were the Leeds family and the Lippencot family. Both of them had a son old enough to be in the hotel business, but only the Leeds' son was into what was going on. Turns out my friend Helen started dating him.

"Elva?" Helen asked, peeking her head into my room.

"Hi, Helen."

"What are you doing tonight?" she asked.

"Tonight? Nothing. Why?"

"Well, Bob and I were going to go out, but one of his friends is in town, so…"

That would be Bob Leeds, son of the owners of the hotel where we worked.

"You need someone to eliminate the third wheel?"

She laughed.

"Something like that. Will you come along? He's a squash pro."

She smiled, and then I had to laugh.

"Of course," I said. "Sounds lovely. What time?"

"8:30?"

So after dinner I quickly got dressed and met Helen downstairs. Then we went outside and met up with Bob Leeds and his squash-playing friend. That's when they pulled up in the Leeds' limosine. I looked at Helen and we both smiled.

"What are you girls waiting for?" Bob asked, opening the door.

Late that night we put the limo in the garage and then they walked us to the door of the hotel where we stayed. It was well after midnight which meant we'd have to sign in and then face the stern matron in the morning.

Oh well, I thought. *It was worth it.*

But when we walked up to the door, Bob just opened it and then looked deliberately at the night man.

"Good evening, Harry," he said.

"Good evening, Mr. Leeds," the night man said.

And we didn't sign in.

"I guess you don't have to sign in when you're with the right people," I whispered to Helen, and we laughed all the way to our rooms.

CHAPTER TEN

Steel Pier in Atlantic City was known as the "Showplace of the Nation." In the 1920s they had performers like John Philip Sousa and Hawaiian hula singers. Gertrude Ederle, the first woman to swim the English Channel, became their first "big" name presenter. The first human cannonball performed there in 1929, along with "Dutchy" Wilde, "the world's greatest daredevil." He jumped into the ocean from a low-flying airplane…without a parachute.

By the time I arrived in the second half of the 30s, the names were getting bigger. The comedians Abbot and Costello performed at Steel Pier. Benny Goodman and Tommy Dorsey brought their famous big bands. Even the Three Stooges appeared. In 1939, a few years after I left, a no-name singer debuted with the Harry James Band for the Easter crowd. The singer's name? Frank Sinatra.[1]

The Steel Pier, especially on the nights when the big bands performed, was a wonderful place. The lights shone into the night sky and the music simply lifted me off my feet. Us girls would walk down there from our boarding hotel and dance the night away. We'd go out on to the dance floor and it never took long for someone to ask you to dance.

If they weren't a very good dancer or there was something I

---

[1] http://www.down-the-shore.com/steelpiertime.html

didn't like about them, I excused myself to go to the bathroom. I'd walk out one of the many doors that surrounded the dance hall, then come back in another door and get a different dance partner. The music was loud and wonderful, and most of the boys were nice and excellent dancers.

The music ended at 11 o'clock and we stood there and clapped and clapped for the band, then walked outside, sad to see another night to its close. On some nights, when the surf was rough, I could hear the waves crashing on the beach. Those of us from the hotel always met outside and walked back together under the stars, and the boys would go with us, making sure that we'd get back okay.

At the end of the summer, when a lot of the people were leaving to go home or find other work, one of the boys I had known came up to me.

"Elva, I wanted to ask you on a date all summer, but I never had the courage."

I just smiled and wished him the best. I don't know what my attitude was back then, or why he wouldn't have asked me. Maybe he was shy – maybe I was intimidating. I don't know. I wasn't attracted to him, but I do remember that he was an excellent dancer.

I could go home in the winter, when things were slower, and I took a Greyhound Bus to get there. Workers were electrifying the Pennsylvania Railroad at that time from Philadelphia to Pittsburgh, and apparently Columbia was a hub for some of the work being done, so there was a large group of workers you'd see, new faces, men who wouldn't be there for long before they would get moved on to another stretch of railroad.

When I came back to Columbia, I felt so much more grown up – now that I had seen the world, Columbia felt like a tiny little provincial place. I had a very close friend who was a few years younger than me. She was still a senior in high school. She had gotten acquainted with some of these men working the railroad, and they were a good crew, a fun bunch of very nice young men. We started hanging out with them in the evenings and on weekends, not really pairing off on dates but just doing stuff as a group. If anyone had a car and somewhere to go, we'd all hop in.

When I hear the kind of stuff that goes on right now, the kind of stuff that kids get into, I just shake my head. We were just babes in the woods back then, so innocent compared to today. But it was a different time, I guess. I just can't imagine doing the stuff you read about nowadays.

One night one of the boys was talking to my friend.

"Hey," he said, "my boss would like to hang out with us one evening. Maybe the four of us could go out?"

"What do you think, Elva?" she said to me.

"What difference does it make?" I said. "Sure. Why not."

So we picked a night and the four of us went out to a restaurant along the highway just south of Lancaster. That's where you went if you wanted to dance, I guess. It wasn't anything like the Steel Pier in Atlantic City, but it was good fun. I was sort of with the guy we knew – his name was Johnny. My friend was with the new guy, the boss that came along. Eventually the boss asked me to dance.

In those days everyone called me "Red" because my hair had some natural, red highlights in it. Elva was a name that everyone always seemed to have a problem with, so Red it was. The boss I was dancing with? They called him Bill.

"Red," Bill said, "you're pretty good at dancing. You're good company."

I smiled. He was kind of a sweet talker.

"I heard one of the other guys call you Norris," I said. "So what's your name? Bill or Norris?"

He smiled.

53

"Most of the guys call me Bill on the job. When I first met my superintendant, he asked me what my name was. I said, 'My name's Norris.' Well, he didn't think Norris was a good name for a boss. 'We'll call you Bill-boy,' my superintendant said. So that's why they call me Bill."

We laughed.

"Well, I think I'll call you Norris, if that's your real name."

He laughed again. We kept dancing for a little while, and before we finished, he asked me out.

"Why don't you and I have a date one night?" he asked. "Just the two of us."

"Okay," I said.

"You tell me when," he said.

I knew that Johnny, the guy I was there with, went home on the weekends. He was sort of the head instigator in our group, and I didn't want to upset him. It's not that we were serious or exclusive – he lived in Harrisburg, and I figured he dated someone else on the weekends when he was out there.

"How about Saturday night?" I asked.

He looked disappointed.

"Aw, Red, darn, that's about the only night that doesn't work."

I thought for a moment, then shrugged.

"Well, that's the only night I can make it," I said.

"You sure do play hard ball, Red," he said.

He thought for a moment.

"Okay," he said. "You're on."

So we went on a date the next weekend. Turns out Norris was a foreman and was responsible for a crew. I don't remember too much about it. Soon I headed back to Atlantic City, and he kept in contact with me. That summer, he made a trip down to see me. It would be my last summer in Atlantic City.

CHAPTER ELEVEN

Norris came down to Atlantic City to see me. By then he had finished the job he had been working on with the railroad and had moved back in with his parents on their farm in Oxford, Pennsylvania, just until something else came up with his company. I was excited to see him. But back then wasn't like it is today, with email and texting and cell phones. I guess we might have talked on the phone.

So when he came down, it was good. It didn't take long for him to share the reason for his visit.

"Why don't we get married, Red?" he said.

That caught me off guard.

"Where will we live?" I asked. "What will we do?"

"I've got it all figured out," Norris said. "My mother pays people to help her around the house – why can't you help her out? My parents have a beautiful home and my mother has these things she likes to get involved in on the side. We could live with them for a little while, just until my next job comes through."

By this time it was 1938 and it still wasn't a great time, especially when it came to finding jobs and getting paid. None of that had changed. Norris was helping his father with their dairy cattle until more work turned up.

I didn't know what to say, and, to be honest, I don't think I thought too long and hard about it. You didn't think about these things very deeply back then – we were mired in practicality, entrenched in a Great Depression, and living from one day to the next. There was sort of this pattern that everyone assumed a woman would follow, and the path involved getting as much school as you could manage, then getting married and having children. There was no expectation at all that a woman would enter into any kind of long-term employment. Of course, most women tried to find work if they could, but that was because they had to, not because they wanted to. Or that was the thinking, anyway.

We went to Elkton and got married – we went there because you could get married on a Sunday in Elkton – and then we drove straight to his parents' farm. I didn't give any notice at work, just packed up my things and left Atlantic City. Even though I was leaving the beach and Steel Pier, it was all very exciting, another adventure.

Can you imagine what Norris's mother must have thought when her 27-year-old son came home with a 19-year-old bride she hadn't known anything about until that moment? Sunday afternoon he explained his plan to his mother. Sunday night we moved into Norris's bedroom, and that was it. The beginning of my married life.

I don't know what my expectations were regarding when I would start working. My expectations were kind of irrelevant though, because on Monday morning Norris's mother came knocking on our door.

"It's Monday," she said through the door. "It's wash day. Time to get up."

I have to admit, for a moment I wondered what I had gotten into. I was not a housework kind of person. I was a work in a glitzy hotel and then go dancing at Steel Pier kind of person. But Norris and I were in love and I was ready to start a new life, so I pulled myself out from under the covers and followed his mother downstairs. Thus began my lesson in the art of keeping house.

His mother was a very unique individual, and it took us a little while to get on good terms, but eventually we became good friends. She was a straight-laced little Quaker lady, and I don't know that Norris had ever had any serious relationships with any other girls before he brought me home. What would I have done if, twenty years later, one of my sons had shown up at the door with a new bride he had only met months before and had married without telling me anything about it until after the fact? I don't know. I hope I would have been as gracious as Norris's mother was with me.

As the days passed, I realized she was good to work with. She was an excellent cook and enjoyed decorating their house and was a very smart woman. She had been in the Quaker church for a long time, but by the time I met her she was a Christian Scientist, so when breakfast was over she spent an hour doing her readings, and it got me interested in it, so I did that for a little while, too.

She was thrilled when I decided to follow in her religious footsteps, and she bought me a leather bound Bible and a Christian Science manual. Her estimation of me grew over the years so that we got to be good friends. She was very fond of me and, as the years passed, she loved the grandchildren as well.

About a week after we got married, Norris and I drove out to Columbia and told my parents. I didn't care too much about what they thought; I had been pretty much in control of my own life ever since my step-father moved in. Something about him marrying my mother sent me off on my own path. My little brother Charlie was nine years old at the time, and he and Norris got on very well. We only spent a day there and then drove back to Norris's family farm. It was already starting to feel more and more like home.

Not long after we were married, Norris's mother went to visit a friend in Philadelphia and left me to take over all of the duties associated with running the house, including cooking all the meals for my father-in-law and Norris. I don't think I even knew how to make a cup of tea at that time. You'd think that after working in a fancy hotel for two summer seasons, I'd have picked up a few pointers on cooking, but while I had learned how to serve with the best of them, I still couldn't cook.

She left me with two men who were busy farming and working up massive appetites. They were milking cows and feeding animals and cleaning out barns and all that, so I was chief cook and bottle washer. They certainly didn't have time to make their own food, and I felt quite a bit of pressure to have everything on the table and ready by the time they came inside.

The guys favorite breakfast was dried-beef gravy, and I knew what time they'd be back in for breakfast, so I decided to try to make dried-beef gravy for them. They milked all morning and usually came in around 8:00 or 8:30am. I got the bacon and eggs ready, but the dried-beef gravy was a real challenge. You had to put the dried beef in and move it around, then you had to add milk and turn it into gravy.

Mine didn't make gravy. I don't know what the problem was. So I put the skillet aside and finished up the bacon and eggs. Then I looked back at the skillet, and it was unsalvageable: a thick paste of overcooked milk and gooey dried beef. I snuck out back and gave it to the dog, and the men had to do with plain old bacon and eggs that morning. Eventually I learned how to make dried beef gravy, and I don't think I had to try too many times, but I finally realized it all worked at a certain temperature.

His mother returned and things got back to normal. Laundry, cleaning, cooking: I learned it all from her. My father-in-law would bring in the eggs, then I would wash them and set them aside. A man drove out to the farm in a walk-in grocery truck and I'd sell him the eggs and then purchase things we didn't have, like coffee or sugar or whatever else we needed at the time. I learned how to stock up the cupboards, and the grocer was very helpful. We never went to the grocery store while we lived on the farm – we simply walked into his truck and collected what we needed.

We didn't need much from the grocery truck, though – so much of our food was grown or harvested or butchered right there on the farm. When the men killed a pig we rendered out the pork chops and put them in a jar and then filled that with grease, turned it upside down, and sealed it. We kept the smoked hams waiting in the attic. We canned all sorts of different vegetables. It was a live-off-the-land kind of life, and I became very fond of it.

Norris and I lived with his parents for maybe six to eight months before moving into a tiny little house on our own, one that had been renovated. It was a simple house without running water or an inside bathroom. We didn't even have water in the kitchen; there was a pump just outside the side door, so whenever we needed water to do the laundry, wash dishes, do the cooking, or even just for drinking – I had to go outside and pump a bucket full. But it was a dear, sweet little house, very clean, and it had been newly done over. My mother-in-law even gave us a bedroom suite when we moved, perhaps in celebration of finally getting rid of us. We also purchased several pieces of inexpensive living room furniture and a kitchen cabinet.

That's the house where we lived when our first child was born.

CHAPTER TWELVE

It was hot, one of those summers when you could see the heat coming up off the field in waves. I sat in our new little house, heavily pregnant, fanning myself, biding my time. Norris was hearing rumors of new jobs about to begin, so we were holding on until that happened. In the midst of our uncertainty, and with rumors of a new war in Europe, Larry entered the world.

His birth was so painful. The little, country hospital where I had him didn't even have a delivery room, so I had him right there in my hospital room. The labor was so long and so difficult that I thought I was going to die right there in the bed. I clearly remember the doctor beginning to panic when Larry wouldn't come all the way out, and when nothing else was working, he put his foot up on the bedframe and pulled on the forceps as hard as he could. I just screamed and screamed, until finally Larry came reluctantly into the world.

The next day, one of the nurses brought me some food.

"I heard you yesterday," she said. "When your little boy was born, I could hear you screaming from all the way down the hall."

I looked up at her and raised my eyebrows.

"Do you know why I didn't holler any louder?" I asked her.

"No," she said. "Why?"

"Cause I couldn't," I said, and there may have been a touch of indignation in my voice, that she would come into my room and make a big deal about me being loud through such a difficult labor.

Larry was 7 pounds, 12 ounces, and I breast fed him. He was a wonderful baby, once he finally made his appearance, and I took to mothering right away.

More good news soon after that: the rumors finally became a reality, and Norris got a job on the Pennsylvania turnpike starting that winter at Sidling Hill. His company would build one of the tunnels (Sidling Hill) that took the new highway through the mountains. He went out to look at the job and check out the area, so when we went out together he had already rented an apartment for us. It was one big room with a flat stove that burned soft coal, and you heated your water, heated the "apartment", and cooked, all on that stove. It didn't take too many cold nights to realize that it wouldn't work for us – it really was a primitive situation – especially with a baby. It simply got too cold, and I couldn't cook on the stove. We lasted one week.

That weekend we went east, bought a house trailer, and then took it back out to the job site. We parked it at the west end of the tunnel, where Norris's company was boring through the mountain – it was a former CCC site, and there was still a building back there where the young men had lived while they built trails through the forest. There was another trailer there with another woman, and we became friends. Behind us, in the forest, there were all sorts of trails. We were just up the trail from the men's bunkhouse, and that's where the water was. Norris carried all of our water up from there. All the water we used came from that bunkhouse.

The front of our trailer had a bunk on each side, and then on the end of that, under the window, was a little chest and a leaf that came out to make a table. One night, when Larry was sick, I put him on one of the bunks and propped myself up on the other bunk and watched him sleep all night, until the forest began to light up and morning crept in through the small windows.

He had a serious cold, and Norris came down from the tunnel during the night to make sure he was okay. He was sick all weekend but we couldn't get to the doctor because the snow was so deep and the roads hadn't been cleared. I prayed and prayed that Larry would be okay. His cough sounded terrible and he ran a pretty high fever. By Monday, the roads were cleared so we raced him to the doctor, but of course by that time Larry was looking perfectly well. We got into the doctor's office, and Larry just bounced on my knee and pushed himself up and down. He was back to his old self, and I felt kind of silly even being there at the doctor's office.

"There isn't a thing wrong with this baby," the doctor said, smiling, and he sent us on our way.

After a few months, a boarder moved in with us – his name was Charlie Murphy from Baltimore. The back end of the trailer had a big double bed, and that's where Norris, the baby, and I slept. Charlie slept up at the front of the trailer in one of the bunks, and on the weekends he went to Baltimore. He was quite a character. He sat around and sang all the time.

I've got a gal in Balt-ee-more
The streetcar runs right by her door
If I had a girly and you had none
I'd make my girly give you some

He was just a funny man.

I packed lunches for Charlie and Norris, and we only went to the grocery once a week. The butcher came to the work site once a week and I bought enough meat for a week. Norris put a box up on a tree and it had a little brass thing you could put a stopper in, and during the winter we put our meat up in the box and it would freeze solid. Wouldn't you know that one day Norris opened the box and some animal had opened the box and eaten everything. I guess we were really out there in the wilderness on that job.

Norris managed to find me a collapsible baby carriage for Larry, so when the winter thawed and spring cleared out all the trails in the woods, I started wheeling Larry through all the forest trails. They had been cleared by the Civilian Conservation Corps during the Depression, but it still made for difficult pushing, especially when the ground was soft – then the little wheels sort of sunk in to the ground. But it was good exercise, and I enjoyed walking through nature, so I often took Larry in the baby carriage through the trails in the woods, and from there I watched the men pouring concrete and building the road to the tunnel.

Later I heard that a local sheriff had showed up one evening at the bunk house and was shooting the breeze with the fellows around the fire.

"I saw the strangest tracks in the woods today," he told the men, and they all sat right up. There were all kinds of rumors about what lived in the endless woods of Central Pennsylvania. Big Foot? Some other fantastical creature?

"There were two sets," the sheriff continued. "Wherever one went, the other went. Just as straight as you please."

One of the men laughed.

"Oh, that's just Boyd's wife," he said, and everyone else burst out laughing. "She goes walking around everywhere with that baby carriage."

It was 1939 and Batman made his first appearance in a comic book, John Steinbeck's *East of Eden* was published, and the world was on the brink of World War II. Later that year, Germany would invade Poland as the world watched in horror.

In the midst of all that was going on in the world, I was all of 20 years old. There were only the two of us women in the entire camp. I hung clothes out in the morning and the fellows drove by on their way to work and they'd all wave and say, "Good morning, Mrs. Boyd," and they were always respectful. I'm sure some of that had to do with Norris being one of the bosses, but I always appreciated how they treated Larry and me.

One day the gal from the other trailer came over and we decided to go for a walk. We got to a part of the stream that was still sort of iced over, somewhere in the shadows of the rocks and the trees. We decided not to take the baby carriage across, but I wanted to see what it was like on the other side of the creek, so I crawled over on a log and just stood there in the quiet, listening.

I looked back over at the other woman standing there with Larry in his stroller. Then I looked deep into the woods. Small drifts of snow still stood in the shadows, and I wondered when was the last time that someone walked through those trees: 50 years ago? 100 years ago? 1000? It was a strange moment, and it really stands out in my mind for some reason. It felt so primitive, like prehistory.

Then I suddenly thought, *What would I do if I saw a bear right now?* So I crawled back across the log, the cold water slipping silently under the ice, and I gripped the stroller, and I was back in modern times. We walked back to the camp through the crisp air and the cold turning to Spring.

The job at Sidling Hill didn't last long, and by later that spring another opportunity came up for Norris. He was doing well, and the upper management folks at his company were starting to notice him. When Arundel Corp landed a big job in Puerto Rico building an airport, Norris got the call.

CHAPTER THIRTEEN

It wasn't a terribly difficult decision, so Norris headed to Puerto Rico while Larry and I moved into a boarding house close to his sister. I wasn't sure if I wanted to go to Puerto Rico; I decided to wait until Norris saw what it was all about. We communicated by letters in those days, and Norris kept asking me when I was going to join him. I kept dragging my heels. Going to Atlantic City as a young single girl was one thing. Moving all the way to Puerto Rico with a baby was a completely different proposition.

I used all of the stall tactics I could. Finally he wrote me a letter saying in no uncertain terms what he expected.

Get yourself on the SS Barbara. If you're not on the Barbara when she arrives here, then I'll be on her when she comes back up to Maryland, and I'll bring you down myself.

I didn't want Norris to have to take all of that time just to come and get me, so I booked a spot on the SS Barbara, a freighter that left out of Baltimore and sailed to San Juan with materials for Arundel Corp. It hauled about 35 passengers, all wives and children relocating to the island of Puerto Rico while their husbands and fathers worked on the new airport there. Larry was ten months old at the time, and everyone made a huge fuss over him. I bought myself a steamer trunk and took his high chair on to the Barbara and kept it in the dining room. I shared a state room with another woman – she had the top bunk and I slept in the bottom bunk with Larry. I guess he must have done pretty well on the boat because I don't remember him making much of a fuss. It was a pretty straightforward journey.

It took about a week to get down there, and I wasn't scared at all during the trip, at least not until I looked down on to the port in San Juan at all the foreigners and thought, *Dear God, what will I do if Norris doesn't show up?* It was total chaos, with people running here and there and workers unloading the boat and sailors heading off into the city. We didn't have cell phones in those days, and I hadn't spoken with Norris on the phone for weeks.

But he was there. It was so good to see his face looking up at me in the middle of that sea of people.

Norris drove me to the edge of San Juan, to a suburb called Santurce, which was a lovely little location. We could walk to a private beach that was sort of like a club attended by the Arundel Corp women as well as some of the wealthier Puerto Rican women, sitting in the sand under their umbrellas. The breeze came up off the blue water, and the palm trees danced around us.

Our apartment was in a large steel and concrete building that contained six apartments. We had one of the apartments on the first floor with minimalist living conditions: it was made up of a living room, a bathroom, and then the building narrowed in and there was a dining room. There was no bedroom – we slept on a pull-out bed in the living room, just off the tiny kitchen. Larry slept in a crib in the dining room. If you woke up at night and went towards the kitchen, you could hear the cockroaches go scurrying in every direction. We "cooked" on a gas stove that you "fed" quarters.

Most of the Arundel Corp men worked afternoon shifts since it was a little cooler during that part of the day, so they'd head off after lunch and then work until 11pm. It was quite an airport back then and would eventually become one of the busiest in the region. Twenty years later, it was from this airport that the famous baseball player Roberto Clemente's plane would take off and then crash. They were on a relief flight headed to Nicaragua. Neither the plane nor any of the bodies would ever be recovered.

Since the men worked in the afternoon and into the evening, this left all of us gals with the children, so we spent the afternoons at the beach and then ate dinner alone in our apartment. It was a nice little community there, and I made a lot of friends.

Larry hadn't started walking yet, but as soon as we stepped foot on the sand he crawled like anything to get to the water. The women sat under umbrellas and played parcheesi – why we played parcheesi, I don't remember. I haven't played it before or since. There was another little child there about Larry's age, and her name was Ann. She had her second birthday there, and Larry had started walking around that time, so the two of them toddled around on the beach and pulled each other's hair and were generally good little buddies. I remember buying a gift for her for her birthday, a fancy little box full of hair bows, and she carried that around for a long time, wherever she went. Of course, we had no idea at the time what an important role Ann would play later in the life of our family.

We had a Puerto Rican maid who came with the apartment. Every morning she walked in and kicked off her shoes right inside the front door, then did her routine. She had an old piece of towel that she used to clean the tile and concrete floors. The windows had screens on them that opened in, and as soon as she came into the apartment she walked over to those screens and opened them wide. I could never understand why she did this.

"No, no, no," I said, trying to explain to her that the screens kept the bugs out. But she just looked at me while I talked and fanned herself, and when I finished she explained herself.

"Hot, hot, hot," she said, as if having the screens closed made her hot. Then she bustled off to some other part of the apartment and performed her routine.

On Sunday evening our maid's sister came to babysit Larry so that Norris and I could go out to eat. Norris made good money, especially considering the year and the cost of living in Puerto Rico, so we'd go to a restaurant and have dinner on the weekends as often as we could – those were really nice nights out on the town. The maid's sister always brought one of her children along when she babysat Larry. Her child was nine years old or so, and I kind of wondered why she did that. Later I learned that if she traveled alone at night, she would be considered a prostitute, so she brought her son along because just his presence kept her safe on their walk home.

There were so many aspects to that culture that took me time to get used to. I soon discovered, after my first trip to market, that Larry was a real curiosity – they didn't have any other white babies around, besides those the Arundel families brought with them. So when I got on the bus to go shopping in San Juan, everyone wanted to touch him, and I let them, but as soon as we got home I gave him a bath and scoured him until his skin was pink.

We didn't stay in Puerto Rico very long. I got there sometime in June and in November we came home for hunting season because Norris didn't like the job that much anyway. When we arrived back in the States, we bought a brand new Plymouth convertible for about seven or eight hundred dollars. My, that was a nice car. It had those perfectly round lights, a front hood that kind of bumped up in the middle, and white-wall tires. We loved taking that car for a spin, the top down, the road and the sky flying past us.

Then Norris went looking for work, all the way to Florida. I think he had a cousin or something there, but I don't think much came of that trip. But we did end up at a Tennesee Valley Authority dam in Tennessee. There was never any housing close to these projects, so we took another trailer there and that's where we lived while he was the master mechanic on the job. We were pretty well taken care of.

You know, Norris may not have finished high school, but that didn't mean he wasn't intelligent. He was brilliant and very mechanically inclined. Everybody who met him, liked him, and this combination of technical ability and a relatable personality had him moving up in the company. Arundel Corp had a lot of different locations, and soon he ended up working right there in a shipyard at Port Deposit. We moved to Millersville, Pennsylvania, and he commuted to work. I guess it took him about an hour to get to work.

We lived in a lovely house in Millersville, built by a professor who had four children. It was on the corner of Kready Avenue, and he had used two lots, landscaping the corner one and building a large two-story brick house on the second lot. He built a smaller Colonial cottage on the back portion of both lots after his four children matured and left the nest. It faced the side street, and was very appropriate for the now-retired couple. He built a detached "dog-house" where he spent most of his time, reading and smoking his ever-present cigar.

I approached him one day with a small maintenance problem and ended up with a resident maintenance man who would accept no pay. When I begged him to let me show my appreciation for his help, he suggested that his favorite cigar store was having a sale, and I might buy him a box when I was downtown.

It was a great arrangement! When I left for meetings or chores, I left the side door unlocked, and when I returned, if there was a strong cigar odor, then I knew our neighbor had been there working in the house. Norris had a wealth of equipment, a lathe, a drill-press, among other things in the basement, and my handyman loved the set up.

Sometime after we moved to Millersville, Norris's father developed kidney problems. We had three children by then, and our youngest, Norris, was in first grade. After my father-in-law died, my mother-in-law sold the farm and moved on to the same street in Millersville, at the other end of the block. My son Norris walked to school, so on his way home he always stopped at his grandmother's house. She kept him well-supplied with either rice pudding or these little almond cookies, so he'd stock up on goodies before making his way home. Then he'd make his way up the street and stop at another mom's house who almost always had sand tart cookies.

Two houses up from us were the Bounds – they had two children who walked to school with Norris: Jimmy and Margie. Before Margie knew what Norris's name was, she called him The Boy because Norris was a big child. She called Norris's father The Boy Daddy. And she called me Dolly. This always made me smile. They were a nice family.

One day, when the children were at school and Norris was at work, I put the milk bottles out on the corner of the tile patio at our back door. I turned to go back inside and tripped up the steps, ramming my hand through the storm door. Glass flew all the way through the kitchen to the dining room, and my arm started gushing blood.

I stared at it for a moment, then wrapped my apron around it, wondering where I could go for help. The lady next door was a very good friend, an older woman, but I knew she would be distraught at the sight of all this blood, so I walked across the street to our other neighbor, a trained nurse. It was a beautiful summer day, and when I got over to her house, the front door was open.

"Charlotte, come here," I shouted into the house.

"Come on in!" Charlotte replied from back in her kitchen.

"I don't think you want me to come in," I said, so she walked towards me.

"I've cut myself," I said, holding the apron tight against my arm, but by that time blood had soaked through and was dripping on to the ground.

"My God," she said, "what do I have that's sterile?"

She looked over her shoulder.

"I know," she said. "I just took some towels off the washline."

She ran to the back and grabbed one, wrapped my arm with it, and then called the doctor.

Norris had already been on the way home from Port Deposit, so when he turned the corner into the neighborhood, she flagged him down and told him what happened.

"Dr. Musselman is in," she said, so he put me in the car and took me to Musselman.

But when the doctor saw the extent of the damage, he passed me on.

"This is not an office job," he said. "You need to get to the hospital."

So Norris drove me in and someone sewed me up and it was a week or two before it had healed enough for me to do anything. They gave me 75 stitches, and it was within a half inch of a main nerve in my elbow. Mother came and cared for me.

I went to a cocktail party with Norris not too long after this. My cuts had healed but it was still a bunch of angry red scars lining my arm, so I bought some long gloves to go with my cocktail dress.

"I heard you cut yourself very badly," one of the women said, curiosity in her voice.

I nodded.

"Yes, it was pretty bad."

She peered at my arm.

"I don't see any evidence of that. It must not have been all that bad."

I pulled off my glove and turned my arm over, and she nearly fainted. I must admit, her reaction kind of made me chuckle.

Eventually, after Norris worked at Port Deposit for some years, they retired the president and made Norris president.

He wasn't only good at the work he did – he was also an excellent father. Of course there were plenty of times when his work took him out of town for short spells. At one point, his company built a fireboat for the Israelis. They built it in Port Deposit and then towed it across the Atlantic and all the way to Haifa to finish it. He took the workmen with him and trained a crew over there on how to operate it.

They also did a lot of work in the country of Colombia. Sometimes he'd have to go down there for a week at a time. I don't think he went there more often than he absolutely had to. Then there was the time he built a gate-lifter in the Great Lakes: we all went with him and lived there for the summer. What a wonderful job. What an exciting time of life, with the children growing older and this feeling that we were moving up in the world, that Norris's hard work was getting him somewhere.

When he did leave us at home, I was in charge of the house. When he came back, the children would cheer and then bombard him with questions.

"Daddy, can we go to the movies tonight?" they asked him.

Can we do this? Can we do that?

"Ask your mother," Norris said.

"For goodness sake, you're their father," I replied. "I think you can tell them whether or not they can go to the movies."

"Yes," he said, "but you're with them all the time. You know if they should be going to the movies. You're in charge."

So we handled his travel pretty well. But I have to admit – when he was working in Port Deposit, and he finally got home at the end of a long day, I always felt a surge of relief.

Oh, thank goodness, Norris is home, I'd think to myself.

He was a good friend.

CHAPTER FOURTEEN

It wasn't too long before Norris tired of the commute from Millersville to Port Deposit, so he bought a lot along a creek and we planned on building a house there that summer so that we could be closer to his work. But we weren't sure that the house would be completed in time for the children to start school in the fall, and we didn't want them going to school for a month in Millersville and then transferring, so Norris sent me down to Hances Point to find a place to rent for the summer and into the fall, by which point we hoped our house would be built.

Someone was designing the house for us, and I had already looked over one set of plans. The house would be right beside a stream, so we had decided to put the bedrooms on the lower floor with the living room upstairs, looking out over the water. The first drawings had already come through, and we had made some changes.

"You go down there and get yourself a real estate man," Norris told me. "Find us a summer cottage. There's lots of water down there, and plenty of houses right off the river and the bay."

So I found a real estate agent.

"I don't have a thing I can even show you right now when it

comes to summer cottages. All of the ones I know about have already been rented for the summer. But there's a house for sale on the Northeast River right in Hances Point. It's where the river joins the bay."

"We already have a plot and a house being designed," I said. "We're only looking for a place to see us through the summer, until the house is ready."

"Well, you're already here," he said. "Since you made the trip down, why don't we go take a look at it?"

"Okay," I said. "I'll look at it. But I hope I'm not wasting your time."

And my time, I thought to myself.

I left my car at Norris's office in Port Deposit and the real estate agent drove us to Hances Point, where we pulled up in front of the biggest, nicest house in the area. It had been built by a man in the building supply business, and everything about it was top notch. We walked up to the door and knocked. A young woman answered the door.

"Hi," my agent said. "We're here to look at the house. Can we come in?"

"I'm sorry," she said. "We have a baby. Can you give me a few minutes before you come in?"

"No problem," the agent said, so I walked around to the other side of the house, just to see what was there. The view was incredible – from that side of the house you could look out over the river, and I just stood there, watching the water drift by. I bought that house in my mind before I even set foot inside.

Then, when I went in, I really fell in love with it. So I went back with the real estate man to get my car at Port Deposit, and before I left I went in to see Norris.

As soon as I walked in, he smiled.

"I've got the second set of drawings," he said. "Do you want to see them?"

"Forget about it," I said. "I just bought a house."

"What?" he exclaimed.

"I said, forget about it. I just bought a house."

"Are you kidding me?"

I shook my head, smiling.

"Well, where is it?" he asked.

"It's at Hances Point," I said. "C'mon, I'll show it to you."

He fell in love with it, too. We stood there in the back yard at Hances Point's highest spot, and we walked down the steps, down, down to the river side. Across the river there were some summer houses and the big club was on that side, the Wellwood Club. Then, up the river, it wasn't very far to the boat yard with its yachts and stores where you could buy boats or boating equipment.

It was a wonderful place.

We bought that house for $27,000, which was a lot of money in those days to pay for a house. The first time we took the children there, they oohed and aahed. If you drove in from the main road, into where the boat yard was, you came up over a hill and then the cottages were a little higher and on the inside of the road was the remains of a golf course.

That summer was lovely, with the children making new friends and running all over Hances Point. Then the bus came in the fall and took them to the schools in Northeast, and winter set in and things got quiet and slightly lonely. The boats took a rest, and the river was quiet, too. Most of the cottages looked at us with empty eyes in the winter, their inhabitants having returned to normal life.

But all in all, we loved Hances Point.

We didn't think the schools in Northeast would give Larry what he needed – he had always required some remedial help when it came to reading. So we put Larry at West Nottingham Academy, and he boarded there until he was 16 and could drive back and forth. I wasn't crazy about the idea of him living away from home, but it wasn't that far, and he was growing up.

That fall, when he turned 16, they had a big dance and the boys were encouraged to take a girl along.

"Larry, have you thought about who you might take to the dance?" I asked him one afternoon.

We had gone to Meadia Heights that summer, to the pool, and he had reconnected with Ann, the little toddler whose parents we had met in Puerto Rico fifteen years earlier, the little girl I had given hair bows to for her 2nd birthday.

"I don't know who to take unless I take that girl who was in Puerto Rico with us," he said. So he asked her and she said yes, and she attended the dance with him and he never had anyone else but Ann. Eventually, a few years later, they were engaged to be married.

Everything seemed to be going so well. My son Norris was enjoying baseball and Laralee was growing up. Norris's job was going better and better, and he started making connections with the higher ups at Arundel Corp. Life moved along, like the river behind our house.

Then came that day in May, when Norris sat on the dock and muttered something about having a "terrible headache," the day I got a call at the house that something had happened to him, that I had to come as quickly as possible. The day I climbed into the back of the ambulance and the driver asked me to hold the oxygen in place while he drove us to the hospital.

I didn't know it at the time, but that would be the day my second life started.

Me in my fancy stroller.

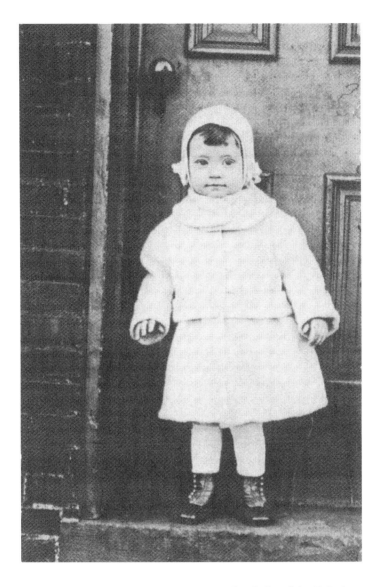

This is me at 902 Houston Street in Columbia, PA, in
approximately 1920.

I'm around 10 years old here with my baby brother, Charles.
Opposite page – My grandfather and me.

Me and Charles.

Opposite – Me with my mom, my step-father, and Charles.

Elva

During my stay in Atlantic City when I was 18 years old.

This is a group picture of the folks I worked with at the hotel in Atlantic City. I'm in the first standing row, second from the right.

My first husband Norris, as a boy.

My husband Norris.

Breaking ground for the Crest of Hershey in a big way. That's me in the driver's seat.

(Opposite Page)
This was the first contract signing with Hershey for 804 apartments. That's me standing to the left, Clyde sitting in the middle, and his brother Abe standing to the right.

Me in the newspaper article about our "Penny-Pincher's Pad."

Cruising.

Dancing with Sandy.

A portrait.

My pastor, Rev. Anne, wearing a stole that I did needlepoint on.

CHAPTER FIFTEEN

I sat there in the back of the ambulance and swayed back and forth as we went around the turns and jumbled up and down over the bumps. I held the oxygen mask on Norris's face and I stared at it. I wondered what was happening. I couldn't imagine he would actually die. I couldn't imagine what that kind of a life would be like.

That's how I rode to the hospital, and he never opened his eyes or stirred at all. I kept willing him to wake up, to come to, to argue with me about going to the hospital. But he never did that. He never moved, and in about twenty minutes we arrived at the hospital, and the ambulance driver managed to get him out of the vehicle and inside the building. I followed along in a daze, and Larry pulled up in his car and joined us.

It was a very small hospital, just a community facility, and they put him in a bed, in a room by himself. The place felt very empty; perhaps they were never very busy, but there weren't many doctors or nurses wandering the halls, and I didn't see any other patients. But maybe that's because I wasn't really looking around all that much, either. I don't know. I think a bomb could have gone off in the vicinity and I might not have noticed it.

Someone checked him in, but I don't remember there being any other staff there to do anything else for him. Someone said he had a hemorrhage and that there was blood way down in his vertabrae. They sent for our family doctor, and it was a little while before he got there. Thirty minutes? An hour? I'm not sure. Time felt different there, in that moment, as if the time I had felt in my life up until then was some kind of artificial time.

Our family doctor arrived, and that made me feel a little better. He had delivered our children, and he knew our family. But his words were not as encouraging as his presence.

"Elva," he said, looking very sad, "Norris has had a massive hemorrhage. There's nothing we can do."

Nothing you can do? I thought. *Nothing you can do? What does that mean?*

He was a big man, our doctor, with a southern accent. Dr. Robinson was his name, and he had dark hair and a fair complexion. Just a wonderful human being. I never had any doctor except him. It must have been hard for him to look at me and say that.

There's nothing we can do.

Meanwhile, Larry shifted in the seat beside me. He had been the one racing the boat, and he had driven his car to the hospital to be with me, following the ambulance from Hances Point. There was nothing the two of us could do but wait. So that's what we did. We waited.

And as we waited, I don't know if it was because Norris was dying or because they were pumping his stomach but my husband kept bringing up more and more of this fried chicken he hadn't completely digested. Not that long ago he had been proclaiming

I don't care if the chicken's done or not! I've got to get the boat out. Let's get dinner on the table!

But now he was lying there, his food coming up, and the doctor said there was nothing we could do. It just felt like a dream, like an impossibility. But it wasn't a dream. It was very real, a fact made even more clear due to the necessity of Larry and me having to unclog the tube emptying the chicken from Norris's stomach. They didn't even have a nurse on duty, so we had to keep clearing the line.

Norris kept dwindling as the minutes and hours passed, and they finally got a private nurse to come in. By then it was around midnight. All I could see through the window was darkness. Someone was home with the children, but I didn't know who. The nurse was a large, crotchety old gal, and she sat there without any sign of emotion on her face, as if she was counting down the minutes until she could go home.

"I wish he would breathe more often," I said to her when I noticed that he was only taking breaths every twenty or thirty seconds.

"Just be happy he's breathing at all," she said sharply.

And that's how Larry and I passed the time, sitting beside this old nurse, waiting. After all of the chicken came up, there wasn't anything left for us to do. Around 4 a.m. I stood up and walked over to Norris again and stood by his head, staring at the wall over his head. I sensed a voice in that silence, speaking to me. Perhaps it was God.

"Are you ready?" the voice asked me, and I knew what the voice was talking about, and I knew what the voice was asking of me. Was I ready to let him go? The question almost sent me reeling.

I took hold of the metal bed frame.

"I'm ready," I whispered. "Go ahead."

Then Norris stopped breathing. I stared at him, the man I loved, the man I married and ran away from Atlantic City with, the man I moved to Sidling Hill and Tennessee and Puerto Rico with. The man whose three children I would now look after.

The man who had been such a good friend to me.

Gone.

The doctor and the nurse moved to the bedside, checked his vitals, and indicated it was over. I turned away and left the room, walked away from Larry and the doctor and the crotchety old nurse and Norris's body, and I drifted down the hall. I walked outside, into what felt like a beautiful, summer evening. But it was so dark, and I walked into the darkness and paced the tree-lined street, amazed and at a loss because of what I had just seen, what had just happened, and I wasn't sure where to go from there.

Then I heard a voice in the darkness, a real flesh-and-blood voice that brought me back to reality.

"Come on inside, Elva," a voice said behind me. I turned, and there stood Dr. Robinson, large and authoritative.

"I just want to be out here," I said quietly, timidly.

"We'll all feel better if you're inside," he explained, and his voice was sad and kind.

I sighed.

"Okay," I said, and with that I returned to the real world, came in out of the shadows and was forced to again confront the death of my husband.

Larry had a car, so we went back home and crawled into bed for a little bit. I don't think I slept. I just lay there under the sheets, staring at the ceiling, very aware of the empty bed beside me. Someone had let Norris's mother and sister know about what had happened, so they were there at the house with Laralee and Norris. We decided not to wake anyone. The kind of news we had to deliver would be best communicated in the light of morning. So Larry and I lay in our beds until the sun came up. Then we told them.

What a situation that was. Norris and I had never talked about dying. He was at the pinnacle of his life, the peak of his career, and death seemed at least 40 years away. It had felt so far off, a worry that we could address in some future time. Suddenly I was bombarded with the realities of death – not just the emotional sense of loss, but all of the hundreds of practical decisions that needed to be made.

I had to decide on who the undertaker would be. We had a good friend who lived in Elkton, where we had gotten married, but that seemed too far away. Norris and I had gone to his father's funeral that the Oxford undertaker had performed, and Norris thought they had done such a good job, so I chose that undertaker.

Of course you have to have a cemetery plot. His family had buried his father in the local cemetery and purchased the adjoining plot for his mother, when she died. There were two additional graves alongside those, so I took one for Norris and the other for me. These are decisions you never think you'll have to make in your thirties. Considerations that seem so far in the future you barely know how to navigate them when they come crashing into your world.

The company that Norris worked for had a head office in New York, and it was a big outfit. My God, the flowers they sent! Wreaths of orchids that drooped down in an open circle followed by baskets and baskets of flowers from every executive and business associate he had. I'm glad they don't do that anymore – it was almost obscene, the number of flowers, the amount of money they must have spent. The small town undertaker didn't have a place to put all the flowers. I can't remember what we did with them all.

Everything seems to happen so quickly in the days following an unexpected death. I was in a haze of disbelief, yet I had so many things to do, so many people to contact and various aspects to organize, and only three days to pull it all together. On the middle day, my friend Betty called me. Her husband worked for Norris and was one of his key employees. Betty and I were good friends.

"Elva," she asked, "what are you going to wear to the funeral?"

"My God, Betty," I said. "I've had so many things to do that I haven't even thought about that."

"All the important people from New York are coming down," she said. "You really need to be appropriately dressed."

I sighed. Shopping was the last thing I felt like doing at that moment.

"You're right," I said. "Of course you're right."

"Get yourself ready," she said in a matter-of-fact tone. "I'll come and get you and we'll go into Wilmington."

So we did. Betty dragged me from one dress shop to another through Wilmington, Delaware. She'd go in and look at what they had and give them an idea of what she wanted. Then she'd come back out.

"They don't have what we're looking for."

Or if something appealed to her, I'd go in and they'd take me to the dressing room and put something over me and she'd say, "Take it off."

Eventually she did find me a very nice dress. It was black embroidered cotton with a little bit of sleeve, and it was just the right dress for Norris's funeral.

That afternoon, as we were dress hunting, I couldn't help but think about all the times that Norris and I and Betty and her husband had entertained these very people from New York, the ones who were now coming down for Norris's funeral. They were a big clique, born and bred in a society far different from ours. Thirty or forty of them would come down to launchings at Port Deposit in a rail car from New York, and they'd bus them to the shipyard and we'd have champagne in the shadow of the barge.

The launching gift would be an engraved bracelet from the Elkton jewelry store, and we'd give it to the person who christened the boat. Then we'd put them all back in the bus and entertain them at the Northeast Yacht Club.

They put on a nice party there, and I'd bring silver to dress up the head table and Betty would bring stuff and we'd do it up right. Betty always had a fascinating memory – she could always tell me which man went with which woman and what their names were. She'd stay right by my elbow the entire time, because as the president of the shipyard's wife, I was supposed to know these things.

"That one with the pink hat is so-and-so's wife," she'd say.

I had a hard time keeping everyone straight.

"Don't worry, Elva," she'd say. "I'll keep you cocked and primed."

And we'd laugh.

As I thought back over those memories during the three days between Norris's death and his funeral, I remembered one trip in particular, when we were still living in Millersville and Norris was commuting to Port Deposit. I remembered heading down to one of those parties, and as I drove down through a beautiful day, to such a beautiful location, I remember thinking something to myself.

"Enjoy this," I thought. "This isn't going to last forever."

But those days were over. I wondered who would take Norris's place. Who would host the parties? Who would move into our house, if we left?

Too many questions. I had enough to worry about in those three short days without adding speculation about the future.

The day of the funeral arrived and it was sunny, blue skies. So many people came that they had to set up chairs outside the funeral home, in the side yard for the employees, and they opened the windows so that everyone could hear the service.

Of course, all the workers from the shipyard came. They had all loved and respected Norris so much, and I could tell they were upset and shocked. Soon, a long line formed to go into see Norris at the viewing, and it was made up mostly of blue-collar guys from Port Deposit. The men didn't have any nice clothes, so they all shared three sport coats. When one of them came back outside, he'd give the sport coat to the next guy in line. They traded it around so that they could wear something nice when they came inside.

I noticed my son Norris, standing off to the side, taking it all in.

When we lived in Millersville we attended a Unitarian church, so we asked the minister from that church to come down and oversee the service. He did a wonderful job. After he finished, we said our last farewells and drove out to the cemetery, where Norris was buried. It was hard watching them lower him into the ground. I was still in shock, and it all felt like a terrible dream.

After the graveside service, they put me in the undertaker's limosine and I sat there, put my head back against the seat. It was over.

Now what?

Then I heard a little tap on the glass. I rolled down my window, and there was a man standing there who I didn't know. I had never seen him before in my life.

"Mrs. Boyd," he said, without introducing himself. "I was very disappointed that you didn't have a masonic service for Norris."

"Oh," I said, rather surprised that someone would have the audacity to be upset with me on the day of my husband's funeral. "I'm sorry."

I never thought anything about a Masonic service. I'm not sure that I even knew there was such a thing. But the man wasn't finished.

"What did you do with his ring?" he asked.

"His ring?"

"Yes, his Masonic ring," the man said.

"It's his ring," I said, starting to feel a little defensive. "Where do you think it is? He's got it on."

"You have two sons," the man said. "One of them might become a Mason, and they would have really cherished their father's ring."

"I'm sorry," I said again, but I wasn't feeling very sorry. "It's his ring."

I had never seen that man before, and I never saw him since. I closed my window and the limosine pulled away.

I was so young. 39 years old. As we drove through that beautiful almost-summer day, with the birds singing and the trees waving back and forth in the breeze, I remember wondering to myself.

How do I live after this? How do I get on with life?

CHAPTER SIXTEEN

We had lived in that house for about four years when Norris died. The winter before he passed away, we had decided to have some work done. We closed in what had been a screen porch on the first floor and made a family room out of it, then built a bedroom over it so that each of the children had their own bedroom. The man who did the job was named John.

There wasn't much work for him in the winter at Hances Point, so he said he'd do the work on a cost-plus basis.

"I'll buy the material," he said, "and I'll do the work and keep track of my time records. I'll present those to you each month, and then I'll add 10% at the end for my profit."

John was a lovely person and he worked all winter on that house. He installed a new heat pump, built that extra room, and added a bath and a new roof. The whole house felt like it was new. The project went a little longer than expected, as those things often do, so he was in the final stages when Norris died so suddenly.

Several weeks after the funeral, when I was going through our finances, I called John.

"John, I'm trying to get to the bottom of all this. I need your bills so that I can pay you."

"Okay," he said. "Let me get everything together and I'll send it

105

over."

I received a packet from John – timesheets, bills, invoices for materials and everything he had spent. I sat down to write him a check, and that's when I thought, *I don't see any 10% added on top of everything.*

I called him again.

"John, I'm not finding fault with your invoices," I said. "In fact, everything is very well organized. I'm ready to write the check, but I can't find the 10% added on."

"You won't find that, Elva," he said.

"What do you mean?"

"Under the circumstances, I won't be charging you the profit margin."

I was flabbergasted.

"But John, if I hadn't gone over the invoices carefully, I wouldn't even have known that you did this for me."

"That's all right, Elva," he said. "I would have known."

I immediately put the house on the market, but you don't sell the biggest, most expensive house in a summer community by putting it up for sale in the summer. I don't know that I showed it very many times that season.

When Norris died, we had $22,500 in life insurance. He had only really been getting started in life. So by the time I had the house and the funeral paid off, I really only had social security. Larry was too old to qualify as my dependent, but the other two children did. I could live and take care of myself and the kids on what I got out of Social Security – about $400 a month. I had a heat bill, electricity, food and clothing, but no mortgage to pay, so that was nice. We did very well on that.

So there it was, staring me in the face: Summer. Hances Point filled up like it normally did, with all the families rolling into town for their summer away from home. Everyone being around kind of kept me busy, and allowed me to keep my mind off of Norris's passing, at least most of the time. My kids seemed to be taking it okay, and they were soon off, racing around Hances Point with their summer friends. Everyone had their boats out. The only thing I remember doing that summer was going to some races with my cousin who I was close to.

Besides that, I pretty much just functioned.

Larry and his fiance had already set a date for the wedding, planning it for August of that summer. They had already paid for the reception, but they came to me and asked what I wanted them to do about their wedding.

"Well, what are you willing to do?" I asked them.

"We could wait until maybe October," Larry said.

As soon as Norris died, I knew I wanted to get back to Lancaster.

"I probably won't get the house ready and sold by October," I said, "so you might as well go ahead with your original plans."

So we got through a wedding ceremony in August and it was okay. I still felt like my world was upside-down. September came and the two younger children went off to school and I got them on the bus and went back to bed in my empty house. Norris was gone. Larry was married. The two children were at school. I literally did nothing that entire month. After a couple of weeks I still wasn't feeling well, so I went to the doctor, the same doctor who had been there when Norris died, the same doctor who delivered my babies. I thought maybe I had caught a bug or something.

"Is this nerves?" I asked him. "Or am I sick?"

"Elva," he said, "you have the constitution of a horse. There's something going around, and you might have a touch of it, but I don't think that's the main problem."

"So what's the problem?" I asked him.

"You need a job," he said.

"A job?" I asked. I had never worked anywhere except as a waitress in Atlantic City twenty years before that.

"Yes, a job," he said. "Get yourself a job."

I walked out of his office not sure what to think. A job? Where would I start? What would I do? I couldn't imagine heading out into the world, joining the labor force. Who would take care of the children? I felt overwhelmed at the prospect.

My friend Betty, the same one who had taken me dress-shopping for Norris's funeral, called me after my appointment. She looked after me in those days, checking in on me constantly.

"So how'd you make out at the doctor's this morning?" she asked.

I was still kind of stunned by his "diagnosis."

"He gave me a little something for what's going around," I said.

"Anything else?" she asked.

"Well, yes. He also told me I needed to get a job."

Betty didn't exhibit any of the surprise I had expected of her. In fact, she got right down to business.

"Okay," she said. "Get yourself dressed tomorrow morning and we'll go out and get you a job."

She was a real do-er. The next morning I woke up and got the kids off to school, but instead of going back to bed I took a shower and put on my best business clothes and waited for Betty to come pick me up. She arrived right on time, and I went out, got in her car, and we went job-hunting.

She took me into Elkton on that late fall day, and there was a county organization there that helped people find work. They got me an interview with a company in Elkton that made fuses, reconditioned air compressors, and also fabricated the balloon sections of blimps. Can you think of a company that had three more diverse items? I couldn't. It seemed rather random, and I wasn't all that excited about it.

But they hired me. I got a job there taking over as the secretary to the purchasing agent. When I took over for the previous girl, I could tell that she had been very, very capable, so I thought she was just on vacation and my position there was temporary. After two weeks I went to work and spoke to the office manager in passing.

"Well, I guess Friday will be my last day," I said.

"Oh, no," the office manager said. "What makes you think that?"

"Isn't what's-her-name coming back?"

He smiled.

"Yes, she's coming back," he said. "But she's working downstairs, with the engineers."

"Oh."

"You still have a job if you want it."

So I stayed on. The purchasing agent's name was Dick and he was an extremely nice person. He was also as ineffective as he was nice. His desk always had piles and piles of things stacked up, orders and invoices and other papers that needed to be taken care of. So I started working on those piles one by one. Sometimes I'd have to go downstairs to find the person who received the shipment and approved the invoice. I was chasing people all over the building for those first few weeks, trying to follow the disastrous paper trail left by Dick. But he really was so nice that I couldn't give him a hard time about it.

I had a few other surprises when I first started. I turned my chair towards the typewriter and pushed on the keys, but nothing happened. I wasn't sure what to think of it. I kind of looked around to make sure no one else in the office was watching me – I didn't like not knowing how to do something, and I wanted to figure it out on my own.

"I bet this sun of a gun is electric," I muttered to myself. I had never seen an electric typewriter in my life; I'm not even sure why that thought came to my mind.

If it's electric, it has to have a switch to turn it on.

I started feeling around the back and the sides and found a switch and the whole thing turned on, making all kinds of noise. I looked around, and none of the other six people in the office seemed to notice anything out of place, so I just started typing.

I spent the next few weeks whittling away at Dick's pile until I made it through every stack of paper on his desk. When I had evidence that the material had been received, I would process the invoice for payment and get it off Dick's desk.

There was a nasty little man who ran the whole show. He was slightly mean and rather spiteful. One morning he was in our office getting ready for year-end closing on November 1st, and they had worked all morning organizing everyone's files. The man came over and sat on Dick's desk while talking with one of the other managers.

"I guess you've got all of your stuff straightened out," he said to another man.

"We're ready for the auditors," the manager replied.

"But God knows what's on Dick's desk," he muttered. Well, that man was talking about my responsibilities – it was my job to keep Dick's desk clean, processing the invoices for payment when delivery had been recorded.

I had one of those old metal tanks with heavy drawers. I opened the bottom drawer so that it made a crash, and he jumped to his feet. I pulled out my four file folders and dangled them in front of him.

"This is what's on Dick's desk," I said firmly. "And even these wouldn't be here if someone had actually approved the receipt of these materials."

Then I put the folders back in my desk and slammed the drawer shut. Everyone in the office stared in our direction, wide-eyed.

The little man went from looking dour and spiteful to gleeful.

"That's what we need around here!" he shouted, laughing. "Somebody who knows what they're doing!"

I worked there through the winter. I would put my younger two children off on the bus in the morning before heading to Elkton to work. By January, a president from one of the local banks called me. He had been a good friend of Norris's.

"Ms. Boyd," he said, "I heard you're working over there in Elkton."

"Yes, I am."

"How are things going for you over there?" he asked me.

"I guess they're going okay," I said. I certainly didn't have any complaints, although Dick hadn't gotten any more competent than he had been when I first arrived.

"Ms. Boyd," he said. "Norris was a good friend of mine, and I don't like to see you working in a place like that. We think you should be working in a bank."

"That sounds good to me," I said. "But you do know that I don't know a thing about banking?"

"That's fine," he said. "You just wait and see. We'll make a banker out of you."

So the next day I put in my notice with the main guy who ran all three areas of the company.

"I'm very disappointed, Elva," he said. "You know, if you stayed, you could have Dick's job."

"You know what?" I said. "I don't want Dick's job."

So I left, and I became a bank teller.

CHAPTER SEVENTEEN

That winter I worked at the bank. The first thing they taught me was familiarity with all the various savings accounts, and soon after that I started on as a teller. I was right beside the manager's desk, and my cage was right next to his. I worked there for about three weeks, and then out of the blue I had this alarming thought.

My God, what do I do if someone wants all of my money?

So I asked my manager.

"What do I do if someone comes up and demands all my money?"

He went straight to the point.

"Give it to 'em," he said. "We don't want any dead tellers around here."

No, we certainly don't, I thought to myself.

I think we also had a button we could push under the counter that alerted the state police barracks and that would bring someone. So that answered that question.

In the mean time, I was trying to sell the biggest house in the summer resort, and now it was winter time. I did have one prospect, a man who traveled through the area from time to time.

He would stop in, look around again, and ask me about the price. Again. I had listed it at $40,000 – you could buy a lot of house in those days for that amount.

"It's a beautiful house, Elva," he said before he left. "Would you consider taking less?"

"No," I said. "That's my price."

A few weeks later he stopped by again and we sat by the fireplace and visited for a little bit.

"You haven't changed your mind about the price?" he asked again.

"No, sir, I haven't changed my mind about the price."

He paused, and I could tell he was thinking it through.

"Okay," he said. "I'll give you your price."

"Good," I said.

"One other question. Would you consider leaving some money in the house?"

"Sure," I said. "I'll leave some money in it."

So I gave him a mortgage and it had a good rate of interest on it.

We prepared to make the move back north to Lancaster. I looked forward to getting the kids back into the good Lancaster County schools and reconnecting with our old friends. I think I also looked forward to putting Hances Point behind us. Not that living there had been a terrible thing – not at all, but Norris was gone, and that beautiful little vacation town simply didn't hold the same things for me that it had when we moved down there.

I went to Lancaster and bought a four-bedroom house with two and half baths for the three of us. It might have been a little ambitious of me, not because of the price, but because of the amount of time it took to keep the house up. Plus, the yard was gigantic, and whoever had lived there before us had planted these beautiful gardens all around the house. Most of my spare time was spent taking care of those gardens. Even though it was a lot of work, it did remind me of my father and his little rows of flowers in Columbia when I was a child. I remembered my mother picking the flowers to take to his graveside. I thought a little differently about my mother after Norris died, or at least I thought I understood her in a differen way.

We only lived in that big house for about a year before moving into something a little more our size. I had managed to make money on the sale of those houses, so the next house I was able to buy with cash which meant I didn't have a mortgage. And I was still collecting interest from the man who had bought my house in Hances Point. I was also still collecting $400 a month on Social Security from Norris's death, and that covered my utilities, food, and clothing because I was very careful. I had grown up during the Great Depression, had even overseen our household expenses when I was a girl, and I knew how to make money stretch.

In those days you could buy a house for around $20,000, which I did. I got the kids in the Manheim Township schools, which I thought was important. Larry came to me about that time and said he wanted to go back to school to study engineering, so I helped him with that. He and his wife stayed in an apartment for a little while, and then when he went to school they lived with her parents.

I remembered my doctor's advice from Hances Point to get a job, so I started looking around for something part time.

"Where do you go to find a job in Lancaster County?" I asked a friend.

They directed me to a man named Greg Celia, a job hunter who had an office downtown. I made an appointment, then went in to see him.

"What would you like to do?" he asked.

"I don't know," I said. "I really don't. But I just want something part time for now."

"Well, let's start with this. What have you done?"

"I worked as an assistant at a business that made fuses, reconditioned air compressors, and the balloon sections of blimps," I said.

"That sounds interesting," Greg said smiling.

"It wasn't," I said. "Then I was a bank teller in Perryville for a few months," I said.

None of this sounded very impressive to me. I wondered if Greg would be able to find me a job.

"Oh, and I worked on Fridays and Mondays at the bank."

His eyes widened and he looked at me from across the desk. He was a rather excitable fellow.

"My God, girl, do you realize what you are offering a banker?" he asked. "They'll kiss the hem of your skirt if you work their two busy days and they don't have to pay you the rest of the week. You're in."

So Greg Celia got me a job with the Bank of Lancaster County, and I worked on Friday and Monday. They soon realized I was experienced and didn't mind moving around, so they started sending me to various branches as needed. I filled in for people who were sick or on vacation, and everywhere I went I walked with confidence because I knew, on that day, I was the best thing they had to fill the gap.

Both of my younger children were still living at home when I started working for the Bank of Lancaster County, but my daughter soon graduated and went to Katie Gibbs, a secretarial school. She met Michael and they got married, so it was just Norris and me at home. He played football at Manheim Township and did very well.

By then, with just of the two of us at home, the house was bigger than I needed. I had a girlfriend whose husband died within six months of Norris's passing. He had a heart attack, walked to the hospital, and died there. Her house was too big for her, too. We were good friends and we spent a lot of time together.

We decided to go on a trip, just the two of us, so we hit the road for Chicago in a white convertible she had recently purchased. We chose Chicago because I had recently started studying handwriting analysis. Working in the bank made me very interested in people's signatures, why they wrote the way that they did. I was curious about the practical application, of comparing signatures and seeing if it was the same person, but I was also interested in what someone's signature might be able to tell me about them. It was an interesting field, and I signed up for a course that had a summer seminar at one of the big schools in Chicago. I talked her into driving out with me.

The two of us stopped in Ohio to spend the night, and in the morning I was dressed and out with my little bag in the car, waiting for her. She didn't normally keep me waiting, but that morning she did. As I sat there, I noticed that across the street there were some new buildings and flags flying, so I walked over to see what all the commotion was about. It was a new townhouse development.

I had never heard of rental townhouses. No one in Lancaster had, or at least I had never seen one there. There was no such thing, not out in the suburbs. So I went through the model, got their brochure, and came back to the car and waited a little longer for her. Finally, she came out.

"Where have you been?" I asked.

"Just getting ready," she said. "What's your big hurry?"

I handed her one of the brochures.

"That's what you and I need," I said. "Two bedrooms, and if we each had one that would be all we needed."

So we went to Chicago and had a wonderful time, but I couldn't stop thinking about the townhouses I had seen. I kept thinking that what I needed was something I could rent out. Instead of buying these big houses I had been living in, I would build a duplex of two townhouses, live in half and rent the other half out. I liked buying new furnishings from time to time, and if I had a small business like this then I could load that kind of stuff on to the expense side. It all sounded good to me.

When we got back from Chicago, I started looking around for a place to build my first two townhouses. I found out about a fellow in Neffsville, a Mennonite electrician whose property still had 100 feet of frontage, more than enough for my duplex. He sold the land to me, and I went to Manheim Township to get approvals.

They weren't extremely easy to work with, but through the process I learned that if I went back a little from the road I would actually have room to build 12 townhouses instead of just two.

Twelve instead of two.

My wheels started turning. I could really start making some money from these rentals. I didn't know it at the time, but this was the launching point for everything that I would do in the future. When I look back over my life, and I see where I've ended up today, I have to say that it was never one big decision that got me here – it was a continual willingness to step out, to take a small chance here, a small chance there. Those twelve townhouses were my first big step.

I went to Bogar Lumber and there was a fellow there who would do some engineering. I asked him to lay the townhouses out for me, and we met a few times. Even after I had the plans, I still wasn't sure how to get these townhouses built. I simply had no experience in the building arena, and I wasn't sure exactly where to start.

One day I ran into the man I had bought the lot from. We talked a little bit about business, and he was eager to see how my lot turned out (both out of curiosity and concern, seeing that I was building right beside him).

"How are you coming with your little houses?" he asked. The

townhouses were a novelty to the people in the community.

"I still need to get a price from someone to build them for me," I said. "Do you know of anyone who could help me out?"

"Why don't you try the contractor I work for in New Holland," he said. "His name is Abram F. Horst."

I wrote the man's name down and decided to look up his company. It seemed like such a small thing in the moment, that name. No big deal, right? Just a name scribbled on to a piece of paper. But connecting with Abram and his son Clyde would be something that changed the direction of my life forever.

It's amazing to me when I look back over my life and see the seemingly random intersections, relationships that I stumbled onto. I think back to when I happened to meet Norris, and how I just so happened to cross paths with the realtor who showed me the house. I think about Norris's death, or how I just so happened to stay across the street in Ohio from the townhouses that were open for me to look inside.

All of these moments. It's amazing how they can add up to a life.

I made an appointment with the Horsts and my son Larry came along with me. By then he had a degree in engineering from Penn State at York. We met with Clyde, who was all of about 23 years old at the time. He was Abram's son. I brought my little brochure from Ohio.

"That's what I want to build," I said.

Clyde looked through the brochure, and he was one of the few people who seemed to take me seriously.

"Give me a chance to put some numbers together," he said.

I also met with another Lancaster County builder, a major player in those days, and he had built some apartments in Neffsville as well. He wanted to give me a price, and when we met he handed me three sheets of yellow legal pad paper with the bid written out. I guess I expected something a little more professional, something a little more detailed. I didn't want to get partway into the project and then get some kind of big surprise.

When I went back and met with Clyde Horst for a second time to look through his bid, he handed me a bound and typed report that included the gauge of the rain spouts and the gauge of the steel for the patio. It was extremely detailed, and it was very professional. A real bid. Larry and I walked out of the meeting pretty impressed.

"I don't know who's going to build this for you," Larry said, "but Clyde Horst is the one who would build it for me."

CHAPTER EIGHTEEN

It was 1963, and I gave Clyde the contract.

In the mean time, the bank where I worked was giving their employees low-interest financing to purchase a house, around 3.5% or 4%, very low for those days. I went to them when I wanted to build my townhouses, but they decided not to give me the money. I guess they didn't consider me to be a good risk.

My attorney, Clay Burkholder, sent me to Educator's Insurance Company. They had an office downtown and there was this great big man behind the desk. I told him how much money I had and what I wanted to do.

"No problem," he said. They gave me the loan, and it was around $600 a month. I was approved for the financing. I had what I needed for the down payment, and I guess this fellow from Educator's apparently thought I could do what I said I would do.

Clyde started the project and I went down every once in a while to New Holland to choose from the various types of bricks and other materials. I was impressed with the work they were doing. One day, while I was down there, he made an interesting comment.

"You know, Elva, hardly a week goes by that someone doesn't come in and want me to build more of these townhouses," he said.

"Is that right?" I asked. "I guess they're very practical."

"They're a pretty good deal," he admitted. "And less expensive to build."

He paused for a moment and then continued.

"Would you have any objections to Abe and I using your floor plans if we build more units like this?"

"Where are you going to build them?" I asked.

"In New Holland," he said.

"Oh, go ahead," I said. "That wouldn't be competition for me."

So during one of my next visits he told me that they were building 32 more townhouse units in New Holland while they finished up my 12 units in Neffsville. It was interesting to me to see how these townhouses were really taking off.

"So how's business going, Clyde?" I asked him pretty soon after that.

"We're busy," he said in a matter-of-fact tone. "People just keep calling and asking us to build these townhouses."

"Here's something for you to think about," I said. "The person who bought my house in Hances Point just paid it off, and I borrowed $60,000 to build these 12 townhouses, so I've got some cash left over. If someone calls and wants you to build more townhouses and you're not able to do it, give them my number. I'd be interested in getting involved."

In the mean time, I decided that if I was going to be renting out my townhouses I needed to learn more about being a property manager. I was still working at the Bank of Lancaster County, but I started looking through the job ads for property manager positions. I saw one opening with a large developer that owned a property right here in Lancaster. They had 212 apartments in a new communitcy called Roseville House, and only 12 had been rented so far.

I answered the ad and they asked me to come talk to them, so I drove into Philadelphia, to their headquarters, and applied for the position. They were called National Land and Development Company, and they had apartment buildings all over the East. A month passed after the interview and I didn't hear anything. I assumed they found someone with experience (which I didn't have).

But then they called.

"We would like to offer you the position at Roseville House," the person on the phone said. "Could you be ready to start by Saturday?"

This was on a Wednesday. I was pretty surprised. When I first applied for the position, I thought I had a chance, but as more time passed I became less convinced that I would actually get the job. I had no experience – none. That said, I wasn't intimidated or scared. I was always a pretty confident person, convinced that I could learn what I needed to learn fast enough to do a good job.

I went down the next day and got acquainted with the job, signed all the paperwork, and took a look around. On Saturday morning I met one of the managers from a community in York that they owned, and she spent the morning explaining everything to me. So that was my indoctrination into the world of property management – one Saturday morning, for about two hours. Then she left, and I was the property manager for over 200 units.

I had a good maintenance man there as well – he was quite the joker, and he called me Tweety. The vacant apartments were all closed up without heat or air conditioning, so the parquay floors had warped and raised up. My maintenance man started making his way through all of those apartments, cutting out pieces so the floors could settle back down and then gluing them together. We had a lot of work to do, and a lot of apartments to fix up and get rented out, but I took it as a personal challenge.

In the mean time, I was also renting out my 12 townhouses. Everything I learned there at the apartment complex was transferring well to my plan with the townhouses. Life was very busy.

My superior was a man named Turney Gratz, a great bulldog of a man with a thick southern accent. He rotated through three or four states for National Land and Development Company, and I'd see him every few weeks. When he arrived I pulled out my long list of questions, and he'd answer them each methodically. He was a great guy, very patient, and good to work with.

"What do you do about this?" I asked.

"What do you do about that?"

"What do you do when they want to leave?"

"What do you do when you want them to leave?"

Turney would call and say, "I'm arriving in the afternoon. Get me a room at that hotel on the Lititz Pike. Give me a chance to get settled and then come on over – I'll buy you dinner."

"Don't worry about me for dinner," I said. "I'll take care of my own dinner."

I didn't want to be on that arrangement, so he'd eat his dinner at the hotel restaurant and I'd ask him all of my questions while he ate. He answered in between bites of food. He was a big, heavy man with dark hair and dark eyes. Turney Gratz was a good man, and he taught me a lot in those years about the right way to rent apartments and how to treat your tenants.

When I was still managing at Roseville House, I had a friend pretty high up over at Armstrong named Ed Smith. Ed was part of a department that hired, and there were times when he needed a furnished apartment so he'd call me to see if I had anything available. He would usually bring the person out and I'd get them furniture and fix them up.

One day he called me with a bit of a different request.

"Elva," he said, "we just hired the first black engineer for

Armstrong. This is our first black employee at that level in the company. He needs a place to live."

"Okay," I said, waiting for him to go on.

"Should I bring him out to look at some apartments, or can I send him out?"

"You don't have to bring him out," I said. "Just send him. I'll take care of him."

We still had new apartments that hadn't been lived in. The man arrived and his name was Bill. My office was in a model apartment and I showed him the map of the community with the buildings marked. I had picked one out for him on the corner where he wouldn't have to park in the main, front lot. This was in the '60s and some were very hateful towards black people in those days. I didn't want him to have any trouble with folks who might not be as open to having a black neighbor.

"It's pretty cold out there," I said, "and I don't have anyone to answer the phones. If I give you a map of the complex and give you a key, will you go look at it?"

"Sure," Bill said.

Not too much later, he came back.

"That will do nicely," he said.

He filled out the application and gave me a check for the security deposit. He told me when they'd be moving in.

"Now," he said. "I have a favor to ask of you."

"Of course. Go ahead."

"My wife was very tenderly raised, down in Philadelphia. Her father was a doctor. She doesn't know how ugly the world is," he paused, and I could tell by his voice that there were many levels of meaning to what he was saying. "If you have any problems related to us being in this apartment, let it be Your problem and My problem."

"I got it," I said quietly. "I understand."

That building he lived in was our only really deluxe building. After he moved in, I saw several of the other people who lived in that building, and I asked them how things were going and if anyone was giving him or his wife a hard time.

"Everyone is civil," they told me. "When we see him out and about we say hello, and he says hello to us. He's a very nice man."

Not too long after that, I went to a cocktail party with some old school Lancastrians. One fellow had a mother who lived in the same building as Bill. When she moved in, several months before Bill, her son had put in custom carpet. They spent a lot of time fretting about getting her apartment in perfect condition before she moved in.

Well, I was enjoying myself at this cocktail party when out of nowhere the son of this woman backs me up against the wall. That joker put his finger in my face and hissed some very hateful words at me.

"You brought the first Negro into Manheim Township and I'm going to run you and the Negro both out of town. And I'm getting my mother out of that place," he said in a threatening voice.

But it took more than that to rattle me. I just looked at him calmly, and when he finished speaking I had one thing to say to him before walking away.

"That's fine, but you're not getting your money back on the custom carpet."

Do you know what she objected to? When she heard the toilet flush, she said, she knew "that negro" was using the same toilet system that she was.

A few years after that, once I had left that community and started many other things, I became curious. I got out the telephone directory and, lo and behold, both Bill and that man's mother were both still living in that community. And decades later, after I moved into my apartment in Willow Valley, I realized the man who confronted me was also living there. He had a dear little wife, and he passed away not long after that. Nobody knows this story, but when I'd see him in the dining room, I'd think, *You sucker, you.*

It bothered me that someone would be that narrow-minded, but it didn't intimidate me at all. I could stand up for myself.

Clyde and I stayed in touch during that time. He had just about finished my apartments, but he had also entered the world of townhouse management, so he'd often call me with questions. I also had a ton of supplies from my employers, more leases and applications than I would ever use, so I told Clyde not to worry about that kind of stuff and I'd give him what he needed.

Hardly a week went by that Clyde wasn't calling and asking me about managing apartments. I guess they had gotten in a little over their heads with all of the townhouses they had built. Then he called me one day with an entirely different proposition, something that would propel both of us to the next level in the property world.

"Hershey wants some apartments built up there by the new medical center. They're tearing down some other housing and they need more parking for Hershey Park. The people being displaced don't have anywhere to live, so they want to build around 1,000 apartments that will be affordable for those folks."

1,000 apartments? I thought to myself.

"They have the land set aside for the builders to use," he said.

"Really?" I asked, my mind racing.

"And they're willing to loan the builder construction funds."

I could hardly contain myself. The two most difficult parts of any project like that was obtaining the land and acquiring the finance. And Clyde was telling me that those two things not only were taken care of but would be paid for by the customer.

"My God, Clyde, do you know what you've just been offered?"

"No," he said. "Do you think we should go talk to them?"

CHAPTER NINETEEN

We went hand in hand to put in a proposal at Hershey in 1967, just four years after I first built my own set of townhouses. Clyde was young enough to be my son, and we had developed a kind of friendship during those early years. Even at that age, he was an expert in construction, and I was quickly learning a lot about managing apartments. Independently, we had been acquiring the skills we needed to form an effective partnership.

Hershey was expanding quickly – the Medical Center was being built, the park was expanding, and they had saved 50 acres along the highway into town and close to the Medical Center for housing. Dr. Hershey gave us the plot plan of the 50 acre site, and he walked out with us. We would need to show exactly where we would build, and how we would arrange the buildings.

Neither Clyde nor I had much experience in the apartment design field. The development I was managing had two-story buildings, with four doors together in the middle – two were to the first floor apartments, and two opened to the individual staircases which gave access to the apartments on the second floor. Those stairs were the responsibility of the tenant on the second floor. These seemed appropriate for families with children. Roseville

House also had three-story buildings, which we used for adults. We had also seen a small one-bedroom apartment in a construction magazine which he thought was very neat. It had the living room and bedroom on the larger outside wall, and the entry and kitchen on the smaller side.

Our first presentation to Dr. John Hershey had a combination of those three different styles – the multi-storied building was to be for adults, the two-stories for families, and the others for single adults. But we did have them all sort of connected, and when we showed it to John he laughed.

"This looks like a motel. You can do better than this."

We walked out both discouraged and hopeful. Discouraged because our first plan hadn't been good enough; hopeful because John Hershey had proposals coming in from huge developers in Baltimore and Philadelphia, developers who were desperate for this project, yet John liked us and wanted to work with us. I think the fact that Clyde would build them and I would manage them (from an apartment I lived at on site) appealed to them.

Clyde and I walked outside after that first meeting, and then Clyde handed me the rolled-up plans.

"I don't have anyone to work on this layout," he said. "See what you can do with it."

I was dumb-struck! But I could also see that if we were going to get any further with this project, I would have to make something that we could present to Dr. Hershey. I took the plans home and spread them out on my table. I'm pretty sure at some point during that process I thought about the fact that I had graduated from high school with a commercial course – I didn't have a college degree in engineering. I had never done anything like that before. But that didn't really bother me.

I started with a fresh plan and made cut out templates of the apartment buildings. I laid out the 130 apartments with one street going straight through and then little side streets that were all dead ends. It looked like a Christmas tree. The side streets were all two-story apartments for families with children, and then at the end was the three-story building for adults only.

We took our new plan back to Hershey.

They liked it.

We got the contract.

It was a pretty amazing set up for a small group like ours because we didn't have to have any financing – we simply had to do a good job building and managing the property. On the first of each month Clyde called me and told me how much Horst Construction would need that month, and then I'd call the president of the bank.

"Al, we need $250,000 this month for construction costs."

"Okay, Elva. Do you want it by the tenth?"

"That's right," I'd say, and he'd get me the money by the tenth of the month.

That's how we built 800 apartments over the next several years in Hershey. We were building all the time. The first section was all garden apartments and the second section was townhouses, which by that time had become rather popular. The third section was three four-story buildings for adults only. Clyde had found someone who would do the architectural design and I would go to his office in Reading to pick up the plans.

I became the main contact between the Hershey folks and the company owned by Clyde, Abe and I – we named it Clabel Corporation by incorporating the first two letters of each of our names. John Hershey and I became very good friends. In later years, after I remarried, John and his wife would often have dinner with us or we'd go up to their house and sit on his porch and just talk. They lived in the house that Milton Hershey had lived in, right along the highway in the outskirts of everything going on up there. John had such a lovely wife. It was a pleasant relationship, and John was a wonderful man to work with.

John was in his 60s at that point. He had dark hair and was always a little on the heavy side. He was very polished and always wore suits and white shirts. He and his wife had gone to a college somewhere in Illinois or Indiana, I believe, and they had first started for Hershey as house parents at the school. He had come in by train and had an appointment with Milton Hershey.

"I had really hoped to interview both you and your wife," Milton told John.

"I couldn't afford to bring my wife," John said. "You'll have to believe we'll be good houseparents."

Milton hired them, and they were Milton Hershey's first houseparents. They climbed the ladder from there.

Our contract with Hershey required us to pay them a portion of each rented apartment, and that number varied from month to month based on the occupancy rate. So every month we paid them an amount based on how many tenants we had in the building. There was a stipulation in the contract that allowed them to audit our books at any point to make sure we were giving them the right number, but they never checked. Not once. They had confidence in us, and we never fibbed on one apartment – they had given us the opportunity of a lifetime, and we didn't want to mess that up.

Our company, Clabel, started looking around for other projects to add to our holdings. The apartments in Hershey were a great foundation for us, both in solidifying our cash flow and in giving us something to point potential investors to as a model of how we did business and could manage a large number of units. About that time, the village of Old Hickory came up as a foreclosure, and Clyde got a group of investors together to front the money for us to purchase the 132 apartments.

We purchased Old Hickory the day before it was supposed to

be sold at a sheriff's sale. That settlement lasted all day, and I think there were something like 13 attorneys there because the previous owners had run out of money before it was completed and all the contractors were being represented, hoping they could get paid. We had to get something done before the courthouse closed, and I think we ended up closing on the property around 9pm that night.

So I started going back and forth to Hershey and I had a desk in the corner of Hershey's real estate office downtown. I rented the first 75 apartments in Hershey using a looseleaf notebook with floor plans and a carpet binder. But it wasn't all about me – the people up there were very underserved when it came to available apartments, so they were looking for places to live. Besides, we had Hershey's blessing and their assurance that we would be watched by Hershey.

Several of those early buildings were three-story walk-ups. You walked in the entrance and could go down one flight of steps to a lower level, or you could go up a flight to the second level, or you could go up two flights to the upper level. We thought we'd put older people in those apartments and not children.

Then we had the two-story ones where we put the families, and those included washer-dryers. When some of the older folks saw those floor plans, they really wanted them because of the washer-dryers, so I told Clyde we were making a mistake by not putting washer-dryers in the three-story walk-ups.

"Are you sure?" he asked me.

"We need to redesign those three-stories to have washer-dryers," I said.

"I'll have to increase the contract," he said hesitantly.

"Whatever you need to do, do it," I said.

Those are the kinds of things I was able to do because I was on the job, saw the challenges first-hand, and could come up with solutions. The more apartments and townhouses that I saw, the more astute I became at being able to picture the eventual layout and identify problems. It was something I enjoyed quite a bit, and the business was growing. I hardly recognized myself as the same woman who had gone to the doctor only to be told, "You need to get a job." Those sad, slow days after Norris's death had been replaced with a fast-paced life, something I could really sink my teeth into.

I made periodic trips to Hershey to discuss our progress as we built this massive project which yielded 804 apartments.

We were almost finished, and I had gone to Hershey to discuss some things with John in his office. As our meeting wound down, John's voice took on a serious tone.

"Elva, what are you going to do when you get a black applicant?"

"Oh, John," I said, smiling, and adding in my best Southern drawl, "Don't look so concerned. We's integrated."

He sort of jumped in his seat.

"Tell me about it."

"Well, you know the three-story apartments where we only put adults? If we have a black couple come in to rent, we show them a floor that has all four apartments vacant. Then, when we rent the other three, say we have a couple coming to look, we say, 'You can have this apartment here or this one across the hall, but I do want you to know that you'll have a black neighbor. Will that be a problem?'"

"Have you had any problems?" John asked.

"None," I said. "99% of the people we ask say they don't mind it at all. These are open-minded people, John."

That's how we integrated our apartments. It wasn't legal then, to ask people if they're okay living next to a minority, and it's not legal today. You couldn't tell your staff to do something like that, but if they were smart, they'd figure it out. If they had a whole lot of apartments to rent, they'd find a way.

John was pretty tickled that I had accomplished it because Hershey had thirty or so different entities at that point and integration had been a bit of a problem for some of them. It might be hard to believe, but that was a big deal back then, and I was glad to have managed it.

We finally signed a mortgage agreement with Hershey for the whole deal, worth millions of dollars, and I wanted to be well-dressed for this meeting so I went to one of the nicer stores and found myself a brown dress. Brown at Hershey was always great. The dress was very tailored with white down the front and nice buttons. It was a very good looking dress. It was the only time Clyde ever remarked on anything that I wore – our relationship was all business.

After the signing, he said to me, "That's a pretty dress you have on."

"It should be," I said. "It's the most expensive dress I ever bought. It cost me $275."

That was a lot of money back then, especially for a dress.

"My wife has never had a dress like that," Clyde said.

"That's all right," I said. "She'll learn."

Every once in a while, Clyde and I made a trip around to look at new apartments that other people had built, just to see what other folks were up to and to hopefully get some good design and construction ideas. We were building six communities at that point – Clyde had a lot of Mennonite investors, and we had a track record by then, something that allowed us to raise capital when we needed it.

Sometimes when we went on these trips, I would come from Neffsville and he would come from New Holland and we'd meet at the Lancaster Shopping Center where I would join him in his car. I pulled in to the parking lot and he was there waiting for me. Every so often I'd catch someone's face who saw me get out of my car and then climb into his car, and they stared. I guess it looked a little suspicious, even though I was old enough to be his mother. That always made me laugh.

We even went on trips with the GE company to Hawaii – we bought so many appliances through them that I guess we were a pretty big customer. At another time, we went to Philadelphia where GE was trying out a new clothes washer. I was supposed to demonstrate how handy it was. So we went on trips like that together.

I wouldn't say that Clyde and I had a close relationship, although we had a lot of appreciation for each other's skills. He was a top-notch builder, and I like to think he considered me to be a top-notch manager with an eye for how an apartment should be laid out. For a time, we made a great team.

At times we would have rental problems. Once, when a new road was being built that isolated our new project, we created an advertising gimmick called a Penny-Pincher's Pad: for $600 we furnished an entire apartment. The dining room table was a door on sawhorses, we bought used furniture and the headboard in the master bedroom was a kitty gate. Garvin's was selling out and we had a manequin, so we took off one of the arms and turned it into a towel rack in the bathroom. We figured that a young couple, if they were both handy, they could do the same thing we did.

It got us a full page in the Lancaster News. "The Penny-Pincher's Pad. Those are the kinds of things we did in those days, and it usually got us a bump in calls from folks interested in renting one of our apartments.

I was always the liason with Hershey Estates. They trusted me completely, never once excercising their ability to check our numbers. (We paid ground rent for every apartment that was producing rent, and they had the privilege of checking our records at any time, but they never did.)

As we continued to expand, I had many meetings with John Hershey. I would go to John's plush office and we'd work things out. We were nearing completion of the project – 804 apartments. The first section was the garden apartments, the middle section was townhouses, and the last section, which included the large building with our rental office, had a large party room for the use of all of the tenants and a the pool and recreational area on the lower level. The rentals in that section were tall buildings with elevators, and those were for adults only. These buildings faced the Motor Lodge and the street leading to the Medical Center.

We had the first building ready at Hershey and I was preparing to move into the model. I planned on using that as my living quarters but also showing it when I needed to. But something came up that kept me from moving in.

I met Sandy.

CHAPTER TWENTY

I pulled up along the curb and beeped my horn. I was supposed to pick up my friend and take her to a meeting at church, and for some reason I was running a little late, or at least was tight for time. When she didn't come out right away, I got out of my car and walked up to the house.

"Come on in," my friend said, opening the door.

"We're late, Ann," I said. "Aren't you ready?"

"A friend of ours stopped by and I'd like you to meet him," she said.

I walked a little further into the house.

"Elva, this is Sandy," she said. "Sandy, Elva."

"Pleased to meet you," I said, before turning back to Ann. "Ann, c'mon."

She rolled her eyes.

"Okay, okay. Let's go."

On the way to church she kept talking about this Sandy fellow, how he had been divorced for four or five years and went to his mother's house for dinner one night a week which was just across the street from Ann's house.

"He's a very sweet man, Elva. Don't you ever get lonely?"

"I'm too busy to get lonely, Ann."

Maybe that was true, and maybe it wasn't. I certainly didn't spend much time thinking about finding a man – I was so occupied with our new buildings and dealing with emergencies and considering potential properties. I was enjoying life, and it didn't seem like anything was missing from my life.

But when I stopped, for just a moment, and thought about what my friend Ann was suggesting…well, it made me think. It would be fun to share life with someone again. It would be nice to come home to a house that wasn't empty.

Not too much longer after that, Sandy called and asked if I wanted to go up to Ephrata to see the theatrical production of The Sound of Music with him. I wasn't sure about it, but I figured it couldn't hurt to go along. So that was our first date. We went up to Ephrata and walked in and got our seats. It was a very enjoyable show, and at intermission we walked outside to get a drink. He was easy to talk to, and we had a great time learning more about one another. I have to admit, it was a little disarming when I found out that, while I had grandchildren, he had a ten-year-old son.

After intermission, we went back in and found our seats. But before the show started up again, a huge spotlight shone down right where we sat.

What in the world has Sandy done now? I wondered to myself.

A man came from between the curtains.

"We have a man with us tonight," he said in a booming voice, "who has always been responsible for the Sound of Music."

What have I gotten myself into? I didn't like having any attention drawn to me.

I sort of shrunk down in my seat, expecting the worst.

The man with the booming voice continued.

"So we'd like to welcome Fred Waring to the production tonight!"

Fred Waring was sitting right there in front of us; he was a popular radio personality back in those days and a well-known big band leader. Some people referred to him as "America's Singing Master." He stood up in the spotlight and turned to face the audience, waving to everyone before taking his seat.

Meanwhile, I sighed with relief. I looked over at Sandy, and he shrugged. I laughed. It was quite a first date.

The months passed, and we didn't see any reason that we should be alone or that I should live in Hershey. Sandy was Jewish, so we went down to Philadelphia and a rabbi married us. Having been a Unitarian for many years, I decided it wouldn't be a problem for me to convert to Judaism. I could handle how they felt about things, and I thought it would be nice if my husband and I shared the same religious practices.

"I think I'm going to convert to Judaism," I told Sandy one evening.

"You know it doesn't make any difference to me, Elva," he said. "I hope you're not doing it because you feel any pressure from me."

"I know. I know. But I'd like to. Anyway, I've already set up some appointments with your rabbi to give me some instruction on becoming Jewish."

I had three appointments with his rabbi. I would go to his office after closing down whichever one of Clabel's offices I was in that day. It was usually pretty late in the afternoon. I was learning quite a bit, and there didn't seem to be anything in the way of me becoming Jewish.

During my third appointment with the rabbi, we were conversing and he was teaching me. But out of the blue he looked at me and asked me a question.

"Now let's see. What's your name again?"

Something about that turned me off. I felt like I was taking this conversion very seriously, but after that it didn't seem like it mattered very much to the rabbi. I went home that night and told Sandy to forget about me being Jewish. It wasn't going to happen.

"That rabbi has absolutely no enthusiasm about me becoming Jewish," I fumed.

Sandy just shrugged his shoulders.

"That's okay by me," he said.

A few years passed and Sandy I settled into our marriage. The business I ran with the Horsts continued to expand. Soon we had 964 apartments in Hershey, 742 apartments at Pineford in Middletown, and five other smaller developments throughout Lancaster. Things were really humming.

But our advertising costs were escalating. We had ads in nearly every major paper or publication in the area, and we had to run different ads for the different communities based on their location and which newspaper we were marketing them in.

There has to be a cheaper way, I thought. Then I got an idea.

I did one ad for all five communities. The ad showed a map of Lancaster County and instead of identifying the towns where the communities were located, we simply put the names of the communities. We put one phone number on the ad, instead of five, and put a girl in a room taking the calls for all five communities. She'd find out where the person was going to work, whether or not they had children, what kind of schools they were looking for, and then she'd suggest that they check out a particular community.

She even arranged for the visit and the viewing of the apartment so that when these people showed up, the manager already knew their names, information about their family, where they worked, and the best kind of apartment for them. That gal was great on the phone, and our new plan impressed a lot of potential tenants.

Those were the kinds of ideas I was always trying to think up. I only had a commercial high school course. I didn't know anything about renting apartments before I got that job with National Land and Development. But when I ran into an aspect of the job I didn't understand, I figured out a way to learn the things that I needed to learn.

Before we started our business, I didn't know anything about interacting with employees, either. At one point we had 13 different entities that I was responsible for. That's a lot of employees! What did I know? I had to go around to each rental community twice a week because I approved the applications and signed the leases, and during all of those visits I quickly learned one thing about employees: they were people. That might sound obvious, but I don't think a lot of employers treat their employees like people. I'd get into the office and sit in a chair across from them and I could have rushed in and done what I needed to do and then got out. But I didn't. I asked them about their family and we talked about their recent sickness or vacation or whatever, and then after a few minutes I'd start through the applications.

I treated them the way that Turney Gratz had always treated me when I was working for National Land and Development: with respect and kindness. I remembered that when he came into the office, good-natured and helpful, it made my week better, not worse. That's the kind of person I tried to be.

After we finished building the 946 apartments in Hershey, I kept on John Hershey's case about selling me a parcel of 22 acres located in the heart of Hershey. We wanted to build some condominiums there. When I asked him for the 22 acres he wouldn't give them to me.

"First let's see what you can do with the 7 ½ acres down behind the telephone company," he said.

That piece of land had a big sinkhole in it, which is why they had never done anything there. It was a bit of a challenge, and it was kind of a this-for-that deal. I'd be doing John a favor by using some rough land, and then hopefully he would return the favor by letting me build on the other 22 acres. So we built 160 apartments on the small lot and called it Cherry Villas. They were sort of Spanish in design, which is where I got the "villa" part of the name. We tried to operate those from the main location at Briarcrest Gardens, without a designated manager, but that was a disaster. We learned an important lesson at that property – you have to have a manager on site, or you run into all kinds of problems.

Through all of these dealings with Hershey, I got to know several of the men who basically ran the town of Hershey. They always treated me like a cohort, with the utmost respect. Usually, though, I worked with John, and one day, after I'd been working with him for ten years or so, he called me up.

"I'm going to ask you to do me a favor, Elva," he said.

"Sure, what can I do for you, John?"

"We have some older properties up here that we've converted to apartments, and their rent hasn't been updated since the conversion."

"Okay?"

"Basically, I need to raise the rents. I'm asking a gentleman from Harrisburg to inspect them, and I'd like you to go along with him and raise the rents for me."

"So you want me to do your dirty work?" I asked, laughing.

He laughed, too.

"I guess that's one way of putting it, Elva. But have I told you recently that you're my favorite red head?"

I laughed again.

"Okay, okay, John. For you, I'll do it."

It didn't sound like an entirely pleasant thing to do, but it was for John, and we were friends. So I went up and met this fellow from Harrisburg and we knocked on the first door. That's when I figured out what was going on. All these tenants we were raising the rent on were the executives of Hershey, the very men I'd been working with for the last few years! Board members of banks and presidents of townships and the like.

When that first door opened and I saw who the tenant was (one of the men I had worked with regarding financing for our recent development), I almost laughed, and I thought to myself, *John Hershey, you scoundrel.*

The next time I saw John Hershey, I walked straight up to him.

"John Hershey, you son of a gun! You made me raise the rent on all those men I've been working with!" I said. "You really did it this time!"

He really laughed then. I guess he was pretty pleased with himself, that he had been able to keep his hands clean through the whole process.

Not too long after that, Clyde and I went to Allentown to the main Pennsylvania Power and Light (PP&L) headquarters. Our visit had something to do with one of our acquisitions. When we walked in I couldn't believe that Turney Gratz was standing there.

It was like seeing a long-lost friend. I walked over to him and we said hello. We were both very happy to see each other after many years. We spent a few minutes catching up, and then he got a serious look on his face.

"Elva, I need a manager for a community. Do you know anyone?"

I told him I wasn't sure but I'd keep my eyes open.

"I want someone who managed like you did," he said, which was a huge compliment, coming from him. Then he paused before saying, "But damn it, I don't want them to buy the community from me!"

We both laughed again. Turney was a good man.

Those were the growth years of our company, and it was full steam ahead. Clyde and I worked hard, each on our separate sides of the business, and things had gone very well. But all of that was about to change.

CHAPTER TWENTY-ONE

I think at some point in life every partnership hits a rough patch. No matter the character of the people involved, no matter how great the beginning was, there comes a time when it becomes evident that people are moving in different directions, and there's just no point in moving on together.

This was the case with Clyde and me in the late 70s.

Larry had gone to school to study engineering, and he started getting more and more involved in the business. Norris's entire education, almost his entire life, had been fashioned around his desire to be involved with our business as well. I encouraged Larry and Norris's involvement, and it made me happy to think that someday they could be an integral part of running our property company.

About that time, we started a new community, one we built in Harrisburg, and it was the first one that Clyde engineered without me being part of it. He had a business partner who had some money. This man didn't know anything about apartments, but we built that community for him, and then we managed it. I took care of staffing it and putting together the model apartment and the office. I managed it the same way I would have managed any of our other locations.

In those days, Norris took over a small arm of the company where we had designated certain maintenance tasks, the physical part of managing apartments. We had a pool at this new complex, but it wasn't used much because there were maybe twenty apartments rented to people who worked every day. In other words, no one was in the pool, but we still had to staff it, so Norris took care of that.

The landscaper who did the initial layout and implementation for that property was responsible for the installation of the grass and then two mowings – after that, they were off the hook. Well, they had mowed twice but not done any weed-wacking, so the grass around the posts had grown pretty tall and the place looked a mess. Norris asked if he could take the lifeguards that he had hired, the ones sitting around doing nothing, and have them shape things up when there wasn't anyone in the pool. He was told, no, that wouldn't be okay.

I knew the place looked awful. Norris knew the place looked awful. But we didn't have any employees other than these lifeguards.

Soon after these various discussions regarding the look of this new development, Clyde called me.

"Elva," he said, "would you meet me at that new project in Harrisburg on Saturday morning?"

"Sure, Clyde," I said. Things had been a little contentious regarding that property, and I was interested to hear what he had to say. "Is something wrong?"

"Just meet me on Saturday, if you can. We can talk about it then."

So we met at that project fairly early on a summer Saturday morning. We sat side by side in straight chairs facing a table in the office.

"Things are looking pretty rough around here, Elva," he said.

"Yes, they are," I said. "But we've talked about that before and we both know why."

Clyde paused and seemed to gather himself before moving on with what felt less like a conversation and more like a speech he had rehearsed for the last 24 hours.

"My business partner has insisted that I fire Norris," he said.

"What?" I asked, surprised.

"My business partner insists that I fire Norris," he said again. "So that's what I'm going to have to do."

"What are you talking about?" I asked him. "Why would you have to fire Norris?"

"This property is in rough shape, Elva. So my business partner has insisted that I fire Norris."

I just sat there quietly, trying not to explode.

"I love you, Elva," Clyde continued. "I pray for you every night of my life."

At that point I lost it. All of the frustration from the issues we had at that property, plus the idea of Norris losing this job that he had spent so many years preparing for, became too much.

"Clyde," I said, staring straight into his eyes. "Save your prayers. My salvation is in good shape. Actually, with what you're doing here, firing my son in this way, you will need every prayer you can get.

I guess the conversation pretty much went downhill after that.

I left the meeting that day knowing that we would have to go our separate ways. In some ways it was a shame, when you think about how much we had accomplished together. I thought about how Clyde had helped me build some of the first townhouses in Lancaster County, how we had gone on to manage the Hershey project and then many more after that. It had been a good run.

But all good things must come to an end. It was time for a new phase in my life.

Soon after that, everyone agreed. It was time to part ways. Thus began the project we now refer to as "marbles."

You take this one, I'll take that one.

We began the tedious task of dividing up Clabel into two separate companies: my company and Clyde's company. There were three big communities at that point: Briarcrest had 804 units; the Village of Pineford was 742 units; Old Hickory was around 400 units. I gave Clyde Briarcrest and took Old Hickory – it wasn't nearly as many units but there was something about that old community I really loved, and I didn't want to walk away from it.

Then we split up the little ones, one at a time. A lot of the little ones were funded by Clyde's friends, so I tried to stay away from those. Eventually it came down to the Village of Pineford, 742 units. We simply couldn't put it on one list or the other because it skewed the lists too much. So I suggested that we sell Pineford, split the money, and part ways.

Clyde agreed.

One day we were Clabel, and the next we were Boyd Wilson Property Management Co. It didn't seem like a big step to me because we had been managing Clabel all along while Clyde had been actively involved in the financing and construction part.

I was really determined to create a thriving family business that involved my children – they had worked so hard over the years to position themselves to contribute, and I was excited about the idea. It didn't feel like a huge step to integrate my sons because Larry and Norris were successful in their own right. They both felt that the ultimate career for them would be real estate. Larry was interested in hotels while Norris was focused on development. The three of us had reached the perfect intersection where we were ready to begin creating something for the family, something for the future.

We took office space in the original farmhouse at the Village of

Olde Hickory. Soon we were planning a new office building to tie into the commercial portion of the community. It was a three-story barn with a silo. The first floor was occupied by Hinkles Pharmacy, a well known pharmacy from Columbia. Our offices were located on the second and third floors. The building was dedicated to me, and my portrait hangs in the conference room.

Clyde and I both got our new organizations up and running, and everything was going well, but Clyde never did anything about selling Pineford. Having it gave him a rather large management company, and that would have been all right except whenever I drove by it didn't seem that it was being taken care of. I was worried that, if it fell into disrepair, the mortgage holders would start putting pressure on us or even pull the mortgage. Clyde was a stellar builder and good at raising money, but he was never as detailed as I was when it came to managing an apartment complex.

We contacted him and said he needed to either take better care of the property or see that it sold. We eventually found a buyer for the community, and when we started putting pressure on Clyde to sell, he ended up buying me out.

You know, there wasn't anything particularly unpleasant about how Clyde and I parted ways except for that one Saturday morning when Clyde and I had that disagreement about firing Norris. I've always had fond memories of the many years I worked with Clyde, and I've never wished him anything but the best. To me, our parting of ways became nothing more than a business proposition, and it certainly didn't mean that I wanted to stop talking to him.

But you know, these things happen, and life goes on.

After another three or four years, in 1986, Laralee followed her oldest son back to the area and the family business. Her son had come to Lancaster, after graduating from college, to work for me, and Laralee joined him, bringing her two younger sons to Lancaster to make a home here. She had been selling residential real estate in Connecticut for a few years, and we added a residential real estate firm that she ran as a separate company.

During that time, Boyd-Wilson continued to develop in Hershey. Across from Briarcrest Gardens, "THE" Clabell apartment community, sat the 22-acre tract that I still wanted to build condos on. We had been successful with the site behind the telephone company, now called Rosedale, that had satisfied the goal of adding to the Hershey supply of apartments. John Hershey and Boyd-Wilson positioned themselves to give Hershey residents a new and exciting alternative to renting – condominiums. The Crest of Hershey became a townhome community, a New England cottage-style atmosphere – right in the heart of Hershey.

There remained a small subdivision within that community that was waiting to be developed. Laralee changed roles at that time. Her focus became developing that last piece of The Crest. With the guidance of her brothers, this last section was designed, built, and marketed under her direction. There were 32 Carriage Homes that were a happy ending to our lovely Crest of Hershey.

I finally arrived at the dream I had always wanted: I had a family business that involved my children, and they were involved and successful and doing a great job. Everything was moving in the right direction.

CHAPTER TWENTY-TWO

In these busy years, one of the wonderful things I had the opportunity to do was to go to Maine Chance, Arizona, close to Phoenix, to the Elizabeth Arden spa. I'd fly out there and then be driven to the spa, and it was halfway up a large hill, not in the desert but in a sort of green oasis of a place. Apparently Elizabeth Arden, the cosmetics tycoon, had vacationed there. She had horses out there. It was a beautiful place.

The first year I went there, I traveled alone. It was all so new to me, a welcome break from the day-to-day business of managing properties. As I got closer, I was amazed at how isolated it was. There was a main house and a little gate house where the manager lived, but those of us who attended lived in the main house or in one of the side cottages they had built.

I walked into my room, a beautiful little space in the manager's house. It was all pink with a fireplace on one side, and it had originally been designed for Mamie Eisenhower. From there I walked to the main house for dinner, and every part of the day was very structured, and the schedule came in the morning on the breakfast tray. All the activities centered around the main house, the exercise facilities, and the swimming pool.

The second year I went out there, I took Laralee with me, and we shared a room in the main house. When it was time for dinner on that first night, we got dressed up and headed to the dining hall. And when I say dressed up, I mean dressed up. There were no assigned seats, and at that first meal I just so happened to sit at the same table as a Mrs. Yontz from Atlanta, Georgia. She lived in the same neighborhood as Margaret Mitchel, the author of *Gone With the Wind*.

She was a fascinating woman. Every night after that, I tried to sit at the same table as her because she was so flamboyant and interesting and funny. Her clothing was almost like a costume, and her jewelry always matched perfectly. I asked her one evening where she got her clothes, and she told me she had a Japanese dress maker, which was kind of a thing back then among the wealthier people. I had even used a Japanese dressmaker who would travel through Lancaster, stay at The Host hotel, and take appointments. He would measure you there, take a snapshot, and then send your clothes to you.

Mrs. Yontz was older, and she didn't have a great memory, but she was a wonderful storyteller. She was tall, and something about her reminded me of Eleanor Roosevelt. I don't know how much exercising she did or whether or not she came for the physical part of the spa, but she was there every year that I was there. She was very distinguished looking, not what you'd call thin, but not very heavy either and she wore her clothes well.

She didn't even try to remember names – she'd simply call people the name she created for them, usually based on something like where they were from or what they did.

She called me Lancaster, but she pronounced it "Lang-Ca-Stuh" with the deepest of southern accents. She grew up in Virginia wood land and her father was in the lumber business. One evening she turned to me at the dining table.

"Lancaster, do you know my friend BeeBeeMahtin?"

She could be difficult to understand.

"I don't think so, Mrs. Yontz."

She turned away for a moment, perhaps distracted by someone sitting on her other side. She was easily distracted.

But after I thought about it, I realized I did know someone in the lumber business in Lancaster by the name of B.B. Martin.

"Mrs. Yontz," I said. "Are you talking about B.B. Martin?"

"Of course I'm talking about BeeBeeMahtin! Who else would I be talking about? He came to my house, to my father's house, and we youngins would sit around and listen to him. Then, one time in London…"

She went on and on, each story more fascinating and audacious than the one before it. She captivated everyone in the dining hall. It was her stage, and she knew it.

One night at dinner she told me, "Lancaster, if I thought you came to Atlanta and you didn't look me up I would be mortally wounded!"

She made me laugh. Little did she know that I would make a trip to Atlanta for no other reason than to see her!

There were other illustrious people there, and you'd hear rumors about how someone had come into their fortune or who they had been married to. But, besides dinner time, we rarely just sat around and talked. We had a full day of exercises and water aerobics and there was a store where you could purchase clothing and cosmetics. Of course they carried all the Elizabeth Arden products, and the makeup stand was run by a little French girl with a beautiful accent. It was a wonderful experience, made even more wonderful the years that I took my daughter along with me.

On Thursday afternoon we always had a bit of free time, and they'd take us somewhere, maybe to Saks or somewhere else to shop. One time they took us up into the hills, to a very interesting little town. Well, one of the girls on the trip that year had a drinking problem, and when we got back to the bus to return ot Maine Chance, we couldn't find her. I knew to look in a bar, so that's the first place I went, and there she was. She had the most gorgeous piece of jewelry with an intriguing icon on it. I thought that if I was her, I'd be more nervous about getting lost with that beautiful piece of jewelry. I'd be worried that someone would mug me just for that necklace!

Those were our days at Main Chance, when Laralee and I were able to spend some time together. Larry and Norris took care of the business while I was away, and I always returned refreshed and ready for a new challenge.

I'm not sure, though, if I was ready for the passing of my mother.

After my stepfather had passed on, I moved my mother into Brethren Village. She had her own apartment there. Her health declined, and she eventually moved into "nursing care." I was too busy to spend much time with her, but I would try to be there around 5 p.m., when she was served her dinner. Mother wouldn't eat enough if she was left to her own devices. She had trouble getting the food from her plate to her mouth, and she was so worried about soiling her clothes that she'd only take a few bites before giving up.

One Saturday afternoon I went out and we had a nice evening together. We finished with dinner and the nurse came to the room and took away her tray.

She loved Lawrence Welk, so I found the Lawrence Welk show on the television for her – she had trouble operating the remote. I showed her the power button and explained that all she had to do was push it and the television would turn off. She had a roommate who was a little older than her, and bedfast. When I got to the doorway I turned and looked at them both.

"Now you two girls behave yourselves tonight," I said, and they both laughed and assured me that they would be on their best behavior.

"Good night," I said.

The next morning I got a call from the chaplain there at the home. It was early on Sunday.

"You might want to come in earlier today," he said. "Your mother didn't have a very good night.

I got dressed right away and called my brother Charlie to get him to come up from where he lived in Wilmington, Delaware. Then I drove quickly to see Mother.

I walked fast into the facility and down the hall, but when I looked up the chaplain was walking toward me, which I thought was rather odd since it was a Sunday morning and I thought he'd be speaking at a church service somewhere.

He met me there in the hall, took my arm, and gently turned me around.

"Your mother is gone, Elva," he said.

I was stunned.

"Why didn't you tell me sooner?" I asked. "I wanted to be here."

"I didn't think it was going to be that quick. I was with her most of the night, and then I left to get myself dressed for service this morning. By the time I got back to her room, it was all over. I'm very sorry."

I sighed. Mother.

I had begun to think very differently about her in those later years. She was no longer the woman who had moved on from my father so quickly, marrying an abusive man and seeming rather disnterested in my life. No, things had changed. She had become the grandmother to my children and someone I could depend on if I needed help. We had become closer in those later years, and I was sad to think about life without her.

I thought back to my childhood in Columbia, how I left home for Atlantic City without hardly a discussion, how I brought Norris home when we were newly married and she didn't know anything about it. There were things we both could have done differently, I guess, but in the end I was thankful for the relationship we had managed to have, even after those early years.

My mother, Edna Barnes Lowry Lawrence, died in 1980. Life was moving on.

CHAPTER TWENTY-THREE

Back in the early- to mid-80s, it was all the rage to get into hotels. All of us property people just kind of figured that if you could manage apartments, you could manage hotels, because what were they but single-night tenants. Right?

Well, it wasn't that easy. We owned the Quality Inn in New Cumberland, the Old Hickory Inn, and we also had a piece of land in Hershey we were going to turn into the Hershey Holiday Inn. We were nearly ready to close on that, but the bank got cold feet and pulled the financing.

We hired Frank Barrett in the late 80s as a controller of hospitality in order to try and fix the massive bleeding that our hotels had become. Frank had nine years experience working as a CPA with pretty extensive real estate experience, and in his words, he "quickly realized what great apartment managers we were, but hotels weren't our forte." He started trying to convince us to close down the hotels and focus on the rental management side.

After one particularly intense meeting, we finally agreed with Frank. We would get out of the hotel business and get back to what we had always been successful at.

"You realize you just talked yourself out of a job?" Larry told him after the meeting.

Frank shrugged.

"If we make this change, I lose my job. If we don't, the entire company goes under. Doesn't seem like much of a choice to me."

At that point Norris and I decided we wanted to keep this guy. By 1995 Frank was running the day-to-day aspects of the business, overseeing things as we went from around 700 units to just over 3000 units.

Sandy and I started traveling to Florida, and I loved our times there. I even took up golf when I was 71 years old. Now, I never got very good, but I could go out on a Sunday morning and hit the ball around with Sandy. We bought a condo on Marco Island, and there was a sports club there, so we'd go Sunday morning and there were maybe 30 of us retired folks who would hit the course. When we finished golfing we'd go home and get something out of the refrigerator and take it to the isolated beach area that only members could use and have a barbeque. Those were wonderful Sunday afternoons.

The club expanded during that time, and we had a thirteen-member Board of Directors that I served on. There were twelve men and me. There was one young man who was the president of the board, who could have been my son, was a New Englander, and really didn't seem to like the fact that I was on the board. He'd be prone to interrupt the meeting and put all the attention on me. I never understood him.

"Elva, you haven't had much to say this morning. What's on your mind?"

And of course the men gave me all of the difficult things to do, because they didn't want to do them but also because they knew I would do a thorough job. There was a man on the board who used a wheel chair, an attorney who represented the developers. If we wanted to do anything we had to talk to the people in Naples, but they never took me along to Naples – he and the president of the board would go and talk to the officials in Naples, and then they would come back and tell me what Naples had to say. I guess this is what comes of being the only woman on a board.

You know, it was rather unique for a woman to get as involved in business as I had in the 60s, and I was often asked over the years to tell about my accomplishments. I spoke to students at Penn State, at various seminars, and was part of a large committee of developers commissioned to come up with a rental lease for the State of Pennsylvania. By the time I was asked to join the board at Marco Island, I had gotten rather used to the way I was treated as a woman in business.

I always relied on my story about Esther Rosenberg going to heaven to liven up the group.

Esther died and was at the Pearly Gates to gain entry to Heaven. The booming voice said to her, "What was your name on Earth?"

She replied, "I was Esther Rosenberg."

There was a loud turning of the large pages, and the voice said, "I can't find you, Esther. Where did you live on Earth?"

She replied, "With my family in South Philadelphia."

More loud turning of pages.

"I still can't find you, Esther. What did you do on Earth?"

"I collected the rentals on the properties my family owned."

With that, the gates flew open, birds flew around singing, flowers floated down and there was perfume in the air. Esther was dumbfounded.

"Do you do this for everyone?" she asked.

"No," said the booming voice. "You see, we've never had a landlady before!"

One of the board's responsibilities at Marco Island was to establish a building line along the water, and normally it was fifty feet. So you couldn't build a house any closer than fifty feet from the water. I was given the job of overseeing this part of the development, I guess because no one else wanted to do it. It involved telling people "no", which of course meant making some people unhappy. I went down and walked that crazy beach at all hours and tides just so that I could get a feeling for what was fair and right when new houses were being designed and built.

At one point we had an entertainer, a country singer whose name I can't remember. He was young, and he had built himself a house just as you went out from the city of Marco to the coastline and the beginning of the resort. It the first street on the island side of the gatehouse, and it was an amazing house on the water. But he wanted beach front, and there was a lot for sale in our resort, so he bought that lot and had a little house designed that was going to be his beach house.

The question came up as to how far back the house would sit from the water, and of course all eyes on the board turned towards me. Yes, yes, I would take care of it. So I went down to the beach and looked at the lot. That's the first time that I noticed this lot was a wooded lot, and the tree growth went right down towards the beach, much closer than fifty feet. So I contacted whoever had made the submission and told them to have their contractor go down and enclose the area with ropes where they planned to build the house. That way we could get a good picture of where this house would be located.

I then called a Board of Directors meeting on the beach one early morning, and I don't think too many of those men were happy about getting up early and getting their feet wet. I showed them that in his case, we could move the house closer than fifty feet, as long as he kept it in the woods. All those board members walked around with their arms crossed, staring at the crashing waves, trying to look like they knew what I was talking about. In retrospect, I guess it made for a pretty funny scene.

Well, he never ended up building the house, so it was a lot of work for nothing.

"Sandy," I told my husband one night, "I don't know, but I think that board meeting and my recommendation might have rankled the president of the board."

Sandy just laughed. He wasn't really into all the politics of these places, but I always felt like I had good ideas and I enjoyed contributing.

I was wintering there in Florida when I went for a routine colonoscopy. The doctor I had in Florida was a friend of a doctor in Lancaster who we were very close to. When I woke up, the doctor was standing there at my bedside.

"How are you feeling, Elva?" he asked.

"Oh, pretty good," I said.

"Well, I have some good news and some bad news for you," he said. "Which one do you want first?"

"Let's go with the good news first," I said.

"Okay. The upper esophogus we checked is just fine, so that's the good news."

I waited.

"The bad news," he continued, "is that your colon has some polyps, and you're going to need surgery to have them removed."

"Oh," I said. I hated the idea of surgery.

"Here are your options. Today's Friday. You can go home and come back Monday for the surgery, but if you do that you'll have to do the cleanse that you did before your colonoscopy. The other option is that I can get you to the hospital right now and do the surgery straight away."

"That sounds practical," I said. "Let's do it now and get it over with."

So I went out to the car with Sandy and he drove me straight over to the hospital. They did the intake and all sorts of other things, and then the surgeon operated on me. He took out a third of my colon, and everything went very well. One funny thing that happened was that I couldn't eat until my colon had healed enough for me to break wind. Five days after the surgery I was sitting in my bed in the hospital room with Laralee and I turned to her and said, "Did you hear that?"

She laughed and said yes. So I was back to eating.

It turned out that the polyps were cancerous, so I had to go on chemotherapy for six months. Fortunately for me, even at 80 years of age, I had no side affects. I kept my hair and my appetite. Sandy took me in to the oncology unit on Tuesday at 10 a.m. and they hooked me up for chemo. Then Sandy left and went shopping or did something else and came back to pick me up at 2 p.m. I was usually finished and waiting for him.

"What do you want to do now, Elva?" he asked.

I always had the same answer, even though he asked me every time.

"Eat!" I said.

So we went someplace nice for lunch, then back to Marco. It seemed that my chemo was always on a day when there were things going on at the clubhouse, because we'd go in for dinner and my friends would look at me with a strange look on their faces.

"I thought you had chemo today?" someone asked me.

"I did," I said. The chemo just never bothered me at all. I still remember the name of it – Lucavorin. Now it's been fourteen years and I'm still in remission. The last time I went for a colonoscopy, Sandy and I went in and sat down and waited for them to call me in. But then two nurses came out.

"I'm sorry, we didn't see you when you came in, and the doctor is busy. Can you come back tomorrow?"

"Isn't the doctor here today?"

"He's not going to be able to do a colonoscopy on you today," one of the nurses said.

"It's very inconvenient for me to get here," I said. "I really would like to have it done today if at all possible."

So the two of them went back and spoke to the doctor and came back out.

"The doctor has said you don't need to have a colonoscopy anymore, not at your age."

So that was the last time I went in for a colonoscopy.

Immediately after I was discharged from the surgery to remove my polyps, the doctor came in and leafed through his papers. I waited quietly. Then he looked up.

"Do you have any children?" he asked.

"Yes."

"Are they over fifty years old?" he asked.

"Yes, they are."

"Make sure they have colonscopies," he said. "This type of polyp can be a genetic occurrence."

So two of my three children did it pretty quickly, and when they did my older son discovered that he had the same polyps in the same place as mine, where the intestines join the colon. They did surgery on him but they didn't do chemotherapy, something that always bothered me because I had had chemo and it had worked so well in putting the cancer into remission.

I went every six months for updated exams, and I would talk to my oncologyst about my son. He was the head of oncology at the Cleveland Clinic, and then I'd call up north and suggest that Larry get chemo, but he didn't get it until it was too late. Once that cancer began to spread, it was all over.

Larry, my oldest son, died on August 17th, 2004 just a few days shy of his 65th birthday. His passing brought so much pain into our family, and sometimes I still feel like I haven't been able to forgive him for not getting the same treatment that I had. But at the end of the day I know even that would not have guaranteed his survival, and sometimes you just have to move on.

His death did take me back forty years, to the night Norris died. I remembered standing beside him when he took that last breath, then walking out into the darkness. I remembered how the doctor came out and asked me to come back inside.

Life is such a beautiful thing, but sometimes it's so hard, too.

CHAPTER TWENTY-FOUR

John Hershey's wife let Sandy and me know that they were having a big 90th birthday party for John, and even though we were in Florida for the winter, I told Sandy we were going. I still considered John and his wife to be dear friends, and what memories we had! That development in Hershey that Clyde and I had done together had really been the beginning of something big for me and my family. I thought back on all the years I had worked closely with John. I remembered the funny stories. I really wanted to be there with him to celebrate that milestone.

My birthday was the day after John's so I made reservations at Hotel Hershey and set up a birthday brunch for my family to have on my own birthday. It was going to be a good couple of days. Everything was all set and Sandy and I were headed north.

Then I got a call from John's wife. She had taken John to a shopping center and dropped him off at a place where he could wait for her while she parked the car, but by the time she came around again, he had a stroke. They rushed him to the hospital.

The party was called off.

On his birthday, she called again.

"John's gone, Elva," she said. "Not everyone gets to go to heaven on their 90th birthday, but John did."

I was so sad when John passed away. He had been part of such an exciting era in my life, a time when I grew so much as an individual. He gave Clyde and me the opportunity of a life time, and he had also been a dear friend.

You know, the relationship I had with John proves that men and women can work together and have a good relationship. We formed a wonderful business partnership through the years. He was such a good man.

I miss John Hershey.

When you've lived as many years as I have lived, you get to meet all kinds of new and fascinating people. You get to start all kinds of new things – I didn't start golfing until I was in my 70s.

But when you live this many years, you also have to say a lot of good-byes. You have to endure a lot of transitions and a lot of endings. I don't know if it gets any easier or not, the older I get, saying good-bye. I know that Norris's passing was very difficult for me, but I also always had an attitude that, well, you just have to keep going. When my son died, that was a real blow, too. But what can we do? Give up? Stop living?

I guess I've always figured out how to move on, how to keep going. I stay busy. I start new things. I stay involved with my property business. This is life, after all. I want to keep moving forward. I want to keep living.

Sandy played a huge part in my life when it comes to moving forward. He proved to be such a wonderful partner for a second marriage. We had an active social life, either in Lancaster (where, as a native Lancastrian he had attended McCaskey High School and F&M), or in Florida, where we had numerous condos in Naples and Marco Island. Once I took up golf, we especially loved Marco Island where we lived in the golf course community.

At home, in Lancaster, our membership in the Hamilton Club resulted in our particpation in the "Dance of the Month Club," a formal group that met once a month, dressed in formal gowns and tuxedos, and used the old-fashioned "formal dance card method" of assigning partners. Your escort filled your card and those were your dance partners for the evening.

In fact, it didn't matter where our social life took us – we danced!

Soon after we married, Sandy sold the scrap yard his family had owned and got into real estate, forming a partnership "Hetrick, Puffer and Wilson." It was during that time that Sandy and I purchased the Greist Building in downtown Lancaster, spending a lot of time and money trying to bring it up to modern standards. We felt like it was a good move for our property company at the time to own the tallest building in the city – it gave us some good exposure. Eventually we sold out to a younger operator who was better equipped to make it successful.

Sandy and I also built ten modern townhouses on Concord Street, and created lovely modern housing within walking distance of downtown Lancaster. This was the first housing of its kind to be built in the West End, between Chestnut and Walnut Street, and was a nice new addition to the city housing market.

Sandy and I really had such a good life together.

When Sandy got to the place where he wasn't doing very well, I'd go by the full-care facility where he was staying and pick him up. Before I arrived, the nurses got him all dolled up and ready for a night out. Then they'd go get some of the other girls who worked there and show him off.

"Come see Sandy!" they'd say.

It was very pleasant for him, and it was an easy life for him. Sandy's son, Skip, spent a lot of time doing things for his father and made sure that his own son, Adam, got to know his grandfather.

Adam quickly became the apple of Sandy's eye.

But Sandy woke up one Saturday night with trouble breathing, and they took him to the hospital on Sunday morning. As soon as they got him there, they put him on a respirator and that was it. I talked to him a couple hours before he died, and the doctor let me know our options. They said it was over, that he wouldn't live much longer without the respirator. They wanted me to make the decision to turn it off.

"Sandy," I said. "You know what they want me to do."

He said, "Yes," in a barely audible whisper, nodding his head. Even that took a lot of effort.

"You know once we throw that switch, it's all over," I said.

He said yes again. He knew. He talked as well as he could with that respirator on.

"Sandy, you've been lucky," I said, trying not to cry. "You got to see your friends this morning, and your grandson came in from New York. Even your girls from the nursing home came over."

He sort of smiled.

"Not everyone gets to say good-bye, Sandy, but you did."

"I know," he whispered. "I'm happy. I'm happy. I'm happy."

He said that three times. With that, we threw the switch, and it only took a couple of hours before it was all over. Sandy was gone.

I was never what you would call a grieving widow. I simply saw it as a new life, a different phase, a life I was given and one I had to live. I can't say that I ever took any of the things that happened to me extremely hard, at least not to the point of despair. I had to handle things. It was what it was, and I reacted the only way I knew how.

Keep moving forward.

You know, when I think back over my life, I think, *This was a full life. There were some heartaches, but I consider myself very lucky.* I wasn't afraid to take advantage of the things that came up. I made my way with no training, no education, and not much family support when I was young – my family life certainly didn't prepare me for anything that I got into.

Everything happened in a perfect sequence, maybe not how I wanted it to work out, but in hindsight it certainly seems that things worked out the way they should have worked out. Even my parting ways from Clyde – it was obvious that he wasn't going to have either of my sons in the business, and they had both built their lives around being in the business. So even though that was a very difficult thing at the time, now it makes sense to me.

I guess I always felt that I had help with my decisions. I don't want to sound preachy or religious, but if I prayed to myself, when confronted with a tough choice, I'd say, "Lord, make this decision so clear that I can't possibly do anything but the right thing," and it seemed that's always how it went. Then, when I moved back up here after Norris's death, I started going back to church.

I was kind of like the minister's secretary. I'd go in on Wednesdays and do a church bulletin and he was such a wonderful person. I was thinking of all kinds of things I could do to bring in money, being a relatively new single-mother. I knew I needed to do something in the way of making an income because my social security was ending soon.

I'd be in there working, and I'd ask the minister, "What do you think if I'd do so-and-so?"

He'd think about it for a few minutes, and then he'd say, "No, I don't think that's a good idea, Elva." Or he'd say, "Now, I think that idea might have some merit."

Someone asked me years later who I went to for advice, and I said, "My minister."

"Your minister?" they said, sounding surprised.

"Yes, my minister."

"Why do you go to your minister?"

"Well," I told them, "I used to run into my husband's contemporaries, and when I'd talk to them about what I was thinking about doing, their universal answer would be, 'Well, I'd hate to advise you, Elva, because it might not be the right thing for you to do and I don't want to be held responsible.' That's no help. My pastor is always willing to say, 'That's a crazy idea,' or 'That's a great idea!' I think we all need people like that in our lives, people who are willing to give us their honest opinion."

I guess I did come up with my fair share of hair-brained ideas in those days. But a few of them worked pretty well, too.

Speaking of church, we had some good friends, Gil and Ann Twitmire, who were Unitarians, and we often went to church with them. The church had potluck suppers, and one Thursday evening we sat across the table from Hazel Dell Brown, the well known Armstrong decorator. Armstrong had the inside cover page of all of the popular home magazines, like Good Housekeeping, and each month would feature a decorating "miracle" signed by the capable Mrs. Brown.

She looked across the table at us and said, "When are you two going to sign up to be members?"

"Well, actually, no one has put any pressure on us," I said.

She came back quickly with "Now is the time."

So the next Sunday when the call was made, we trotted up to the front of the church, and we signed up.

I soon had the job of arranging flowers in the brass altar vases, mostly from my friends' gardens. When the Christmas season approached, Mrs. Brown chaired the Decorating Committee, and the church looked lovely.

I saw Mrs. Brown downtown, and she asked me what I thought of her efforts. I praised her use of the tiny lights that were new that year – she had amassed live greens on the window sills of our fabulous stained glass windows and they were gorgeous. But I wondered why she had continued to use the large yellow, green, and red bulbs on the two live trees on either side of the chancel. She looked pensive, and didn't answer.

The very next Sunday those big, ugly bulbs had been replaced by the new tiny white ones.

My memory isn't so good anymore, but other than that I'm very lucky. My mind is still sharp, and I stay as involved in the business as I can. When I go to board meetings for my company, I don't always agree with what they want to do, but I try to hold my tongue. During some recent planning meetings, we had some gentleman come up from Philadelphia. I couldn't decide if I was just going to sit there quietly or let them know that I disagreed with them – then I thought, they came all the way up here, so why would I let them go back without knowing that I disagreed with them?

My instincts haven't left me either. I can look at a drawing of a house or an apartment complex and I can tell you if a space works or not. I've always been able to look at architectural renderings and picture in my mind exactly what that space will look like in real life. I don't know where I got that; I don't think it's something you can train or learn, but I've always been able to do it.

I still get all of the financial reports from Boyd-Wilson Property Management, and they are kind enough to involve me in the budgeting meetings. When my son Norris comes into town we'll have a few important meetings, and there's usually a day or two that I need to be involved in, so they'll send someone out to pick me up and take me to the meetings. They don't do very much of anything without giving me an opportunity to help with the decision, and I'm very satisfied with the way they're still including me.

I love our company, not because of the apartments so much as because of the people. I have these people who have worked for me for so long. I'm very proud of our retention rate, our employee status. We have one girl who works for us who is 70 years old. She helps out part time at Old Hickory with rentals. Sometimes these gals who have been at the company for a long time will come and pick me up for lunch. It's all very nice.

We had a Christmas party last year where we gave all the employees a week and a half bonus. We held the party in the second floor of the barn that's been fixed up as a party room. We now have 57 employees, and we also gave each of them a crisp, new $100 bill. Each employee came and sat down in a chair beside me, and I was able to hand out the bills. Of course, we manage communities now that I've never seen, so they each came and sat down and I'd ask them, "Now, tell me who you are and where you work." I'd try to say something pleasant about what they were doing, because everyone in our company works so hard and I appreciate each of them.

We did have one third-generation employee. His grandmother worked for me when we had all these communities. Her name was Shirley, and she was wonderful. She would call the other managers together and run training sessions. Before that, she had gone door to door selling cosmetics, taking care of three children after her divorce. That's all she knew how to do, but she knew how to engage with and manage people, and we made a manager out of her. Then she took over training all the other managers. She died of cancer when she was in her 60s.

Her daughter was raised in our community and she worked for us, and then her son worked in our corporate office in accounting. It's quite a thing. I'm very proud of these old employees. They come and they're happy to be included. I'm very proud of the family feel in our business – it's very satisfying to see what we've managed to grow over the last fifty years or so.

A strong sense of community and family are two of the reasons

I decided, in 2008, to make a $1 million donation to the United Way here in Lancaster. I always wanted to live in Lancaster, even when I was a young girl growing up in Columbia, and I came to love this area dearly. I became involved in the United Way twenty years before, when my son Norris as vice-chair of agency relations and fund distribution.

The United Way became like family to me, and I wanted to make the donation before I died so that I could see with my own eyes how it impacted the community. They say I am the only $1 million-donor at our local United Way. It's hard to believe the little girl who grew up in Columbia would be able to make such a gift, but I guess you never know how things will turn out.

For my 95th birthday I invited forty of my closest friends and relatives to the Lancaster Country Club to have dinner and celebrate along with me. I didn't think I'd ever see my 95th birthday, but that many years seemed like something worth celebrating. Every birthday I have feels like a bigger deal these days, and even though physically I'm not what I used to be, my mind is still sharp and there are few things I enjoy more than a night with friends.

It was beautiful for so many reasons. I got to choose the seating and put some old friends together as well as introduce people who had never met. A lot of things happen through the years, and we've had some family trouble from time to time, but at my 95th birthday some bridges were built and fences mended.

When they brought out my cake, it had "Happy 95th, Elva!" written on it, and there were three candles in each corner. They turned out the lights and the candles really glowed, along with all the cameras that were flashing. Just before I blew the candles out, I looked around in the nearly dark room. So many friends.

What a life.

I made a wish, and I blew the candles out.

Two Stories
By Norris Boyd

I have two stories that I like to tell about my mother, instances that will hopefully give you an idea of how business savvy she still is, even today, at the age of 95. In fact, from a business standpoint, other than the fact that she's not in the office every day, I don't think her savvy is any less than it was twenty years ago.

The first story took place about twenty years ago, when we were talking about doing a deal, and the man we met with was very technical. The group of us were talking with a bunch of bankers, asking questions, what if we do this, what if we do that. Lots of numbers and interest figures and principal amounts flying around the room. And mother would sit there, listening quietly the whole time. Then, when the room grew quiet as the technical guy ran some calculations, Mother piped up.

"I think that's about 6.2%, isn't it?" she said.

And this guy was on his huge calculator typing away furiously, and then, after five minutes or so, he said, "Well, I guess that would be around 6.189%."

Mother was always very sharp with figures. She could run them in her head long before anyone finished typing things into their calculator. I don't know where she got her head for numbers, but that's how she's always been.

The second story took place in more recent years. We were sitting at a table in a conference room, once again talking to bankers. Sometimes things in those meetings get a little boring because it's basically a bunch of guys sitting around trying to impress each other.

One of the men sitting beside me leaned over and nudged me.

"Is Elva okay?" he asked, motioning towards Mother where she sat at the end of the table. She was falling asleep.

"Oh, she's fine," I said. "Nothing's wrong. If you say something interesting, she'll wake up."

She did wake up and she looked around, took a sip of her coffee, and sort of drifted off again.

"Are you sure you don't want to take a break?" the man asked me again. For some reason he was very concerned about Mother.

"No, she's fine," I said. "Watch this."

He sort of sat up straight, and I said the following dollar figure in a firm voice.

"$5,233,147.25."

Mother's eyes opened wide and she leaned forward.

"See," I said. "You start talking about numbers, and she's right here with us."

It's never taken mother long to see through the trash and get to the point. I think that has been one of her greatest strengths over the years. She never hesitates to tell you exactly what she's thinking. She still understands how to get a problem down to its most basic pieces.

Another one of her strengths is that she's not stuck on her own opinion. If you say, "Now, Mother, we're not going to do that because of this," and if your idea makes sense, then she'll change her mind. She's tenacious, and she won't let go of a good idea, but she's not in the least bit stubborn. She's not in the least bit egotistical.

We still use Mother very much as a ground check, as a base check, to make sure that what we're doing makes sense. We have meetings that go into a lot of details, things that she's not privy to anymore, but we still very much value her observations as to what's going on. She helps us to see if we should be where we are, and if we're headed in the right direction.

I marvel at her, at what she's accomplished, and at the person she has become.

Apples, Trees, Mothers, and Daughters
By Laralee Bash

A strong and hearty tree: that would be my Mother. Then there's the "apple that doesn't fall far from the tree": that would be me.

The stories of my Mother's childhood are fascinating to me. Reading her story, I learned some things about her roots that I never knew before. She grew strong and confidant, a product of difficult years, with a real spirit to achieve and a sense of adventure to tackle new opportunities. She was always ready to face life and live it to the fullest.

When she became a Mother, her example for us, her children, was always to figure out "how." She never said, "I can't." She lives her life that way, and we have been taught to do the same.

As you've read, Mother lost her father as a young girl, and her husband as a young wife. That husband she lost was my father, which means I repeated my Mother's story, losing my father at a young age. Then, as if that apple falling was not enough, I repeated history again, losing my husband when I was in my thirties, just as Mother had.

As a family, with Mother at the head, we picked up the pieces of our lives and put them back together to move ahead after my father's death. I had to do the same with my children after the death of their father, following the courage and spirit of Mother. But I did have one advantage: I knew that Mother would be there to pick up the pieces if I needed her to. That knowledge added to my security and my confidence to make a life for my children and myself.

Those were our tragedies.

Mother and I also shared a love of homes and decorating. I remember as a kid we were always excited when we saw a wonderful home we had not seen before, and if it was one that Mother hadn't seen we couldn't wait to share the excitement with her. At Halloween, I always wanted to "trick or treat" at some wonderful house in the neighborhood that I was curious about. Of course, I always tried to see inside.

I definitely got my interest in doing knitting and needlepoint from my Mother. We both have houses full of our projects and have some nice ones to show. As a child, I was never allowed to start a new project before the current one was finished, a trait of stick-to-it-iveness and perseverance that hasn't gone away. We still must finish a piece before we start a new one.

Real estate and development were always a focal point for our family, and it has been a pleasure to be a part of the business that Mother created and shared with my brothers and me. We still love floor plans, picking finishes, decorating models, and even planning communities. What Mother started, we endeavor to grow.

We are proud of our Mother, proud to be a family business. We have a team of employees that we consider family, too, and I'm proud to work together with them, building for the future.

My mother "tree" is 95 and strong today. She continues to set an example of how to grow old gracefully. I can only hope that my story will be half as interesting, and that I can be as sharp as her for many years to come.

Elva

A WRITTEN HEIRLOOM

This book, telling the story of Elva Boyd-Wilson's life, is what I refer to as a Written Heirloom. By taking the time and resources required to have her story preserved in written form, Elva has provided her relatives, descendants, and friends with a valuable resource. The stories of her life will be preserved for many generations to enjoy and learn from.

What will happen to your stories when you are gone?

If you are interested in exploring the idea of creating your own Written Heirloom, please contact me. I'd be happy to send you a free book outlining the process and the cost and answer any questions you might have.

Live a good story.

Shawn Smucker
703 999 4079
shawnsmucker@yahoo.com

49007775R00102

Made in the USA
Charleston, SC
17 November 2015